WARWICK TODD

UP IN THE
BLOCKHOLE

'Cricket's a funny game'
(Inscription found on Roman temple wall, circa 250 AD)

WARWICK TODD

UP IN THE BLOCKHOLE

As told to Damien Todd, who forgot most of it.
And Tom Gleisner, who didn't.

hardie grant books
MELBOURNE · LONDON

Published in 2009 by
Hardie Grant Books
85 High Street
Prahran, Victoria 3181, Australia
www.hardiegrant.com.au

Text © Working Dog Pty Ltd 2009

Cataloguing-in-Publication data is available from the National Library of Australia.
Warwick Todd: Up in the Blockhole
ISBN 978 1 74066 861 3

Cover design by Terkelsen Design
Cover image by Hwa Goh
Text design and typesetting by Terkelsen Design
Printed and bound in Australia by McPherson's Printing Group

10 9 8 7 6 5 4 3 2 1

Dedication

For the three most important people in my life – my children. This book is dedicated to my two wonderful sons, Ian and Greg, and my beautiful daughter Trevor.

Acknowledgements

Disclaimer
This book is not endorsed or in any way approved by or associated with Cricket Australia or any current member of the Australian Cricket Team.

Legal
Will Houghton QC, Greg Sitch

Graphic designer
Rachel Terkelsen

Photographers
Hwa Goh: cover, pp. 9, 14, 26, 27, 32, 35, 36, 37, 38, 39, 40, 43, 47, 49, 51, 59, 60, 65, 67, 68, 73, 75, 78, 80, 91, 95, 98, 100, 101, 103, 105, 109, 111, 113, 129, 149, 157, 177, 188, 189, 190, 191, 192, 197, 213, 215, 223; **Tom Gleisner:** pp. 1, 22, 27, 28, 31, 41, 62, 71, 106, 107, 115, 117, 118, 119, 120, 123, 138, 139, 151, 154, 155, 171, 172, 186, 190, 199; **Shaun McKenna, Image Eight:** pp. 97, 117, 119, 122, 137, 150, 156, 161, 165, 184, 191, 211; **Mary Muirhead:** pp. 77, 93, 132, 216; **Deb Herman:** pp. 58, 74, 125; **Emma McLean:** p. 17; **Carole Burch:** p. 18; **David Herman:** p.18; **John Rudolph:** p. 18; **Sam Gleisner:** p. 99. **Paul Jeffers:** p.169

Additional photographs
Newspix/AFP: p. 52; **Newspix/Brett Costello:** p. 54; **Newspix/AFP:** p. 57; **Newspix/News Ltd:** p. 98; **Newspix/Shannon Morris:** p. 131; **Newspix/Colleen Petch:** pp. 135, 137, 153, 193; **Cluden Cricket Club**, Brighton, Victoria; **Rodney Horin**; **XXXX Gold Beach Cricket (Lion Nathan)**

Composite imaging
Marcus Herman

Production
Production co-ordinator: Deb Herman; 1st AD: Annie Maver; runner: Mark Davis; hair/makeup: Caroline Styles; flicker book images: Phil Simon; production assistant: Michele Burch; financial controller Working Dog: Dan Atkins; photographic assistant: Paul Jeffers

Performers
Sam Gleisner, Annie Gleisner, Ciara McCoppin, Guhan Bala, Jake Lane, Hwa Goh, Bob Maver, Billy Pinnell, Dan Atkins, Rose Hawas, Christine Darcas, Charlie Herman, Harvey Herman, Henry Miller, Mark Davis

Thank you to the following people
Rob Sitch, Santo Cilauro, Michael Hirsh, John Stokes (Cluden Cricket Club President), the past and present members and players of the Cluden Cricket Club, the Rouse Family, Les Pumphrey, Robert Wilkinson, Chris McFadden, Paul Hyland (Glasshaus Nursery), South Yarra 8 to 8 Laundry, Conrad Mace Salon, Aaron Rausch (Retravision, South Yarra), Merrie Harkness, Como Melbourne, Heroes and Legends (Richmond), Melbourne High School Old Boys Association, Neroli Nixon, Pink Ginger, Ripe Studios, Martin Rudolph, Rodney Horin, Sandi Cichello, Jo Blows, 'And special thanks to my good mate Braymien'

Contents

Thanks

I have benefited enormously from the goodwill and support of so many people throughout my career that to mention them all by name would take up several pages, something that would – in turn – mean having to drop a few photographs of me at the crease or cut short some of my match statistics (neither of which is going to happen!), so just consider yourselves all sincerely thanked and let's leave it there. The simple fact is that in a book such as this it's impossible to acknowledge everyone (not to mention foolish, as some of them might start demanding payment). However, a few special people deserve a mention.

First up, special thanks to my wonderful family, in particular Mum and Dad from whom I got my competitive spirit, sense of fair play and eczema. If you ask me, parents are the unsung heroes behind all our sporting stars. When I was a kid they would drive me to matches every weekend, stand on the boundary yelling support and – if we won – drive me home again.

To my brother Damien. We grew up competing together in the backyard and even though I've gone on to achieve greatness on the world sporting stage while you've struggled to hold down a part-time job at Flight Centre you are not a failure, so don't believe all those who constantly say otherwise.

I must also thank my ex-wife Ros – not that she did anything, but it's required under the terms of our divorce settlement. (She also gets 12.5% of recommended retail.)

Thanks to all at Hardie Grant. I think this is one of their finest sports books to date (although, if you've seen some of the other titles currently stacked in the warehouse you'll realise we're starting from a pretty low base).

The following group of creative and hardworking people are deserving of special thanks:

- Neville Gulliver, my Manager
- Deb Herman, my Production Co-ordinator
- The other folks at Hardie Grant who don't seem to do much but come to all the meetings and always have something critical to say.

Finally and above all else, I want to acknowledge the fans. Those die-hard cricket lovers who come to the games, wait outside the rooms for an autograph and who have supported my career ever since I first pulled on the baggy green. I am humbled if I have managed to add some meaning to your otherwise insignificant lives.

Photo acknowledgements

The photos used in the book have been collected from several sources, including professional photographers, spectators, friends and a variety of hidden security cameras. Many have also been taken on tour by team-mates and other members of the squad. Special thanks must go to our physio Alex Kountouris who, knowing I was working on another diary, would often grab my camera and take a few shots, many of which appear in the early parts of the book. This thoughtfulness almost makes up for the fact he later dropped my camera in a hotel pool in Leicester.

Photo courtesy Today Tonight.

Foreword by Ricky Ponting

Subject: Foreword
Date: Thursday, 23 May 2009
From: Sam Halvorsen <smithj@dsegmanagement.com>
To: <wtodd@completelegends.com>
Attachment: Foreword.doc

Hi Warwick,

Ricky has asked me to thank you for your kind invitation for him to provide a foreword for your new book. Unfortunately, due to his tight schedule Ricky is unable to help you out with a personal testimony on this occasion. He has, however, instructed me to forward you the following template that he is happy for you to fill in and use.

Yours truly,
Sam

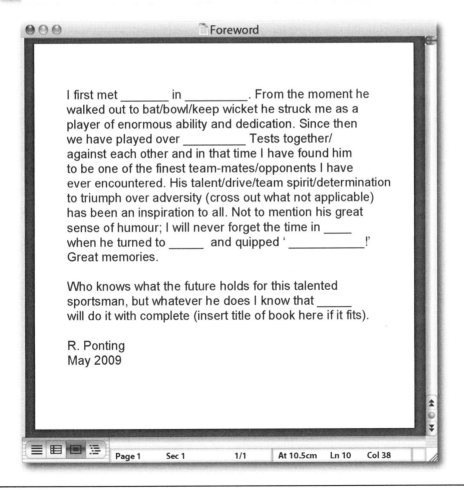

I first met _____ in _____. From the moment he walked out to bat/bowl/keep wicket he struck me as a player of enormous ability and dedication. Since then we have played over _____ Tests together/ against each other and in that time I have found him to be one of the finest team-mates/opponents I have ever encountered. His talent/drive/team spirit/determination to triumph over adversity (cross out what not applicable) has been an inspiration to all. Not to mention his great sense of humour; I will never forget the time in ____ when he turned to _____ and quipped ' _____!' Great memories.

Who knows what the future holds for this talented sportsman, but whatever he does I know that _____ will do it with complete (insert title of book here if it fits).

R. Ponting
May 2009

Page 1   Sec 1   1/1   At 10.5cm   Ln 10   Col 38

About this book

This book is divided into two parts, or three if you count this bit. The first deals with Warwick Todd the cricketer. How did I get to where I am today? What were the influences that shaped my early career? How did this humble country kid with an unorthodox action rise to become one of the modern game's most exciting and heavily sponsored players?

The next section covers my shock retirement and then inspirational re-call to the Australian side for the 2009 Ashes tour. As in past books, I have chosen to go with the diary format. Of course, some cricket diaries tend to focus on little more than ball-by-ball descriptions of the day's play; run after run, dismissal after dismissal. Even for the most ardent fan this can get a little repetitive. Which is why I've also included fielding changes. The hardest thing has been deciding what to leave out. Details of my favourite hotel meals or our tour bus song lists? Complete transcripts of Punter's pre-match briefings or descriptions of our warm-up routines? These elements are all gold and too good to ignore.

But, in addition to daily events, I've attempted to paint a picture of the personalities involved in the game, especially the Australian team members. I realise that, in some cases, this involves lifting the lid on what takes place in the Aussie dressing room and revealing certain incidents that some might feel should be left private. With this in mind, I have, in certain cases, avoided using specific names, preferring anonymous descriptions such as 'a left-handed opening batsman from NSW' or 'greyhound-loving Test captain' to prevent readers identifying any one individual.

Toddy's Take

On various pages you will find boxes like this, headed 'Toddy's Take'. These contain thoughts, musings, reflections and grabs of wisdom that I have collected over the years. Timeless advice like 'don't run on a misfield', 'catches win matches', or 'never leave credit on a drink card'. Simple yet significant guides from a bloke who has seen it all, and remembers bits.

Preface

Attending the 2009 Allan Border Medal. Despite being nominated in several categories I have absolutely no recollection of the event.

Okay, how do you sum up an amazing year in just a few hundred pages? The answer is, you can't, and it's ridiculous to try except for the fact you've signed a publishing deal and already spent most of the advance. So here goes.

No doubt about it, it's been an incredible 12 months for Warwick Todd. Getting divorced, launching my own brand of vodka-based energy drinks, an Australian Taxation Office audit (which, I'm pleased to note, failed to turn up anything *technically* illegal) and – to top it all off – being re-called to the Australian team.

Much has already been written about my shock axing and I certainly don't intend to go over it all again here. But the truth is, I was ready to retire. By the end of 2006 I had lost the 'fire in the belly', that special something that makes us elite athletes want to keep on pushing ourselves to ever greater heights. I'd even raised the idea of retirement with one of my closest team-mates, Matthew Hayden. I remember walking over to Haydos one afternoon and saying, 'Mate, I think it might be time for me to chuck it in.' His reply was typically blunt and to the point: 'We've still got another 27 overs to face, so get your arse back down the other end and take guard.' So I pushed on, but it was a struggle. Yes, the runs kept coming but my general on-field performances began to suffer. The one percenters. A careless snick here, a dropped catch there. A failure to give a departing tail-ender an expletive-laden send-off. I was in danger of letting both myself and the side down. It's funny, I can almost identify the exact moment that I knew for sure my first-class career was over. It was at the end of a Shield match in Brisbane. I got into the rooms and there was a call from Chairman of Selectors Andrew Hilditch saying 'your career's over'.

During my two years out of the game I learned a lot about myself and about life. The importance of slowing down, of savouring each day as it comes. After decades on the road I finally got to spend some quality time with my wife Ros. Our divorce 18 months later was, perhaps, a direct result of this period. Too much quality. And, while we're no longer married, I'm pleased to say we're both still talking, even if it is through our respective lawyers.

Of course, even though I was officially retired, cricket remained a big part of my life. I guess scheduling 63 separate testimonial matches for myself helped me stay in touch with the game. Naturally I kept a close eye on the team, and worried about the string of other experienced players who followed my lead and called it quits. Warnie, Lang, Pigeon, Haydos. Then came a string of losses. To South Africa, followed by New Zealand. So, when Punter called me one afternoon in March '09 and said 'Toddy, we need you back', I was not entirely surprised. But I do remember feeling a range of emotions. Pride, that I could once again be pulling on the precious baggy green. Frustration, that I'd only just sold it on eBay a couple of weeks before. And determination to help lift Australia back to its rightful place as the world's number one team. It didn't take me long to reach a decision. Warwick Todd was back in the squad …

Sporting roots

If you wonder where W. Todd gets his sporting prowess from, you don't have to look far. The Todd family has excelled over the years in a number of sporting fields.

My grandfather Henry Todd was an outstanding sportsman, playing district cricket at A grade level and excelling as a medium-pace bowler. When the First World War broke out he thought nothing of lying about his age (claiming to be 15) but the authorities soon found out and the 23-year-old Henry was shipped off to the Western Front. He was in charge of aiming the heavy artillery and was mentioned in dispatches in 1917 when he managed to wipe out a group of heavily fortified German infantry by getting a shell to reverse swing into their trench. Upon returning Henry continued his cricket career, which, as a result of his wartime injuries, he was able to pursue with both the men's and women's district teams.

Grandma was very much part of the local sporting scene and for years was the official scorer at district games. I can clearly remember sitting next to her on the boundary line and watching as she methodically kept tally of each over, quietly adding a few additional runs to our team's score ('special extras' is what Nan called them) as required. Nan could get pretty vocal, especially by mid-afternoon when the contents of her thermos began to take effect, and in all my years of international cricket I have never heard anything quite as offensive as one of my grandmother's full-on tirades.

My Uncle Doug was an excellent cricketer for our local team where he used to both open the bowling and keep wicket (luckily for Doug he bowled slow). He was also an excellent batsman with a reputation for being tough and gritty, a real hard man of the team. Uncle Doug refused to use gloves or pads as he thought this showed 'gutlessness', and he never wore a protector. He also never had children.

My father Warren could easily have played rugby union for Australia, had he shown the interest, commitment or talent. But cricket was his first love. Dad was a decent off-spinner, as well as a useful batsman, the kind of cricketer everyone wants in their team because he could contribute, but not so much that he was a threat to anyone's place.

Mum was a handy golfer who had she not been banned from club competition for hitting a PGA official with an 8-iron would no doubt have enjoyed even greater success.

Both Dad and Mum were respected members of our local community and I grew up with a strong sense of helping others. Mum would often take in homeless men, and Dad was forever helping police with their inquiries.

Throughout my childhood years my parents were great supporters, and I can clearly remember them both standing on the sidelines, hurling abuse at the opposition and officials whenever they thought my brother or I had been hard done by. This was alright at cricket or football matches, but could get a little embarrassing when they came to watch us in the school play.

Watching me in the Under 17s.

Shakespeare in the Park.

Warwick Donald Todd arrived in the world one wet Thursday morning in October 1968. Mum's waters had broken that morning, something that apparently came as quite a shock to her as up until that time she hadn't realised she was pregnant. A frantic rush to the local hospital produced more dramas when scans suggested I might be in what doctors call the breech position. Turned out I was simply taking block.

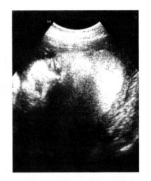

Like generations of Australian kids before me, I was introduced to cricket in the backyard of the family home. But there were no gentle underarm lobs with tennis balls. Dad believed in starting with cricket balls, his only concession being that, prior to us turning three, he would come in off a shortened run-up.

When I was 14 we moved to a larger town and I found myself having to start at a new school. For some reason they must have thought I was pretty smart and I got put in the top class, Year 8A. Within a few weeks they realised their mistake and I was relegated to 8D. By the end of the term I was in Year 7 but still playing for the First XI.

The club years

The Elmhurst Grammar First XI. Our coach Mr Pankhurst (circled) later retired from teaching to become a professional Latin dance instructor. Back row: G. Tollert, B. Crepps, F. Molly, B. Fitzpatrick. Centre: R. Hass, W. Montgomery, P. Farrington, Mr S. Pankhurst (coach), R. Hunt. Front: M. Holbrek, P. Francis, G. Chirrup, A. Hartnett. Absent: W. Todd (suspended).

Cromlee was one of the most successful district teams of the 1970s, in part due to their practice of encouraging every member to impersonate a favourite player. Amongst the 'stars' in our line-up: Max Walker, Garry Gilmour, Len Pascoe, Greg Chappell, Dennis Lillee, and – somewhat inexplicably – Sarfraz Nawaz.

ABOVE LEFT: From an early age I learnt the importance of celebrating a big win. Here some of the boys test out a new team victory anthem, specially penned for big occasions. ABOVE RIGHT: Members of our leadership group read through the team's recently drafted Code of Conduct. It was later rejected when no one could agree on a definition of 'unsportsmanlike conduct'.

My first coach

I can still remember my first coach. His name was Phillip Joyce. But to most of us kids who showed up at his training sessions after school each afternoon, he was simply 'Coach'. Phil was always big on what he called the 'one percenters'. A traditionalist, he felt there's no point in scoring a century if you've got your shirt hanging out. Phil was also a hard task master, with a very clear sense of right and wrong. Once, during a club game, I took an extra orange juice during the lunch break. Phil came up to me after the game and said, 'Woz, did you take that extra orange juice?' I said 'no' but he kept hounding me so eventually I caved in and confessed. He just looked at me with a sort of pained expression before saying, 'Honesty and respect for others matter more than anything in this world.' Interesting words, and ones that came back to me 12 years later when Phil was jailed for obtaining financial advantage by deception.

1.

W. TODD – BACK IN THE SQUAD

May

25 Monday

Pre-Tour Training Camp, Coolum

We arrived at Coolum on the Sunshine Coast today for our pre-tour camp ahead of the Twenty20 and Ashes series. The aim is to recreate tour conditions as closely as possible, which I guess is why we kicked things off with 18 holes of golf.

All but one of the 16-man Ashes squad are here (Huss is still on his way back from South Africa), along with the Twenty20 guys. In addition to us players, partners have been welcomed: wives, girlfriends and a couple of chicks a few of the boys picked up at Coolangatta Airport. It's all part of Cricket Australia's 'family friendly' policy.

As usual on the Sunshine Coast, it was pissing with rain, so most of the day was spent in meetings: contract discussions, sponsorship talks, medicals (a few of the boys thought they might have had swine flu – turned out they were just hung-over).

I tell you what, it's a far cry from the 2006 boot camp when our former coach John Buchanan forced us through four days of 'army style' team-building activities in the surrounding bush. I'm all for 'thinking outside the square', but I'm still not sure about the wisdom of handing fast bowlers a selection of semi-automatic weapons and telling them to 'go find themselves'. From memory, after a night in the rainforest we all just came back cold, wet and pissed off (although Glenn McGrath did manage to shoot a pig).

You could tell everyone was pretty pumped up about the series, keen to get back into action. More than half the squad have never played an Ashes Test, so it falls to experienced players such as Yours Truly to help prepare these rookies for what lies ahead. Injury-wise we're looking in good shape. Bing's ankle has fully recovered, as has Watto's groin. My knee is still a worry. I injured it several weeks ago, during a Cricket Australia counselling session. But I'm confident it's coming good.

The purpose of the camp is largely administrative – handing out tour clothing and equipment and getting police checks done on new players.

On the second day the rain eased off to a gentle torrent and we were able to have a short net session. The facilities here at Coolum are pretty good and the resort staff can provide just about anything. I remember last year Punter was a little concerned about his batting form and so arranged for a giant plasma TV screen to be set up in the practice nets to help him identify his problem. In the end I don't think it helped Punter all that much, but we did get to watch a lot of *Dr Phil*.

James Sutherland, Cricket Australia Chief Executive, gave his usual talk focusing on our continuing commitment to the Spirit of Cricket. This is a code that we have adopted because we recognise we are seen as role models. He pointed out that when travelling overseas we are all effectively ambassadors for our country. A couple of guys asked whether this gave us diplomatic immunity, or free parking, but the answer seemed to be no.

Cricket Australia's receptionist was then asked to address us. She told us about the stress and abuse she experienced when fielding complaints on the phone if any of us stepped out of line. The boys were pretty stunned by this and, after she left the room, we reached a unanimous agreement. They should sack her and get someone in less likely to whinge.

At the meeting tonight Punter spoke to each player individually, put some tour goals in place and got everything ready. He also gave each player a one-page outline of what he expected of them. Here's what he gave me:

Toddy, enjoy the tour – your time is now.
Work with Pup and Huss to really cement our middle order.
Controlled aggression coupled with technique will lead to runs.
Don't be intimidated by the Poms – stand up to them with aggressive body language, looks and words at all opportunities (except maybe during the national anthem or post-match presentations).
Keep the intensity up at fielding practice – take it into the game with you.
Be the man – make it your series.
Play well.
I want my iPod back.
– Punter

Australia's 2009 Ashes squad

Ricky Ponting (c), *Punter*
Michael Clarke (vc), *Pup*
Stuart Clark, *Sarfraz*
Brad Haddin, *BJ*
Nathan Hauritz, *Ritzy*
Ben Hilfenhaus, *Hilfy*
Phillip Hughes, *Boofa*
Michael Hussey, *Huss* or *Mr Cricket*
Simon Katich, *Katto* or *Mrs Cricket*
Mitchell Johnson, *Mitch* or *Midge*
Brett Lee, *Bing* or *Binga*
Graham Manou, *Choco*
Andrew McDonald, *Ronnie*
Marcus North, *Snorks*
Peter Siddle, *Sidds* or *Vicious*
Warwick Todd, *Toddy*
Shane Watson, *Watto* or *Subject to fitness*

ICC World Twenty20 squad

Ricky Ponting (c), *Punter*
Michael Clarke (vc), *Pup*
Nathan Bracken, *Brack* or *Andy G*
Brad Haddin, *BJ*
Nathan Hauritz, *Ritzy*
Ben Hilfenhaus, *Hilfy*
James Hopes, *Catfish*
David Hussey, *Huss*
Mike Hussey, *Huss* or *Mr Cricket*
Mitchell Johnson, *Mitch* or *Midge*
Brett Lee, *Bing* or *Binga* or *Bingo*
Peter Siddle, *Sidds* or *Vicious*
Andrew Symonds, *Roy* or *Symmo*
Warwick Todd, *Toddy*
David Warner, *Lloyd*
Shane Watson, *Watto*

Nicknames are important to Australian team members, but they need to be agreed on well in advance. Back in 2006 we had a near disaster when Brad Hodge and Brad Hogg were named in the squad – and both insisted on the same nickname! Cricket Australia mediators had to be called in to resolve the issue but, despite their best work, it's still simmering.

2009 Pre-Season Goals

Technical
- Batting: drives and bat swing, cuts, pulls
- Bowling: run-up, through the crease
- Fielding: run-outs, diving saves, slips and cover catching

Physical
- Stronger: weights, boxing, agility
- Workouts: Taebok* classes
- Diet: low-carb beer, fruit and vegies (in moderation)
- Tattoo: get rid of 'Ros' from left butt cheek

Mental
- Be the man
- Stay in the zone
- Be positive – avoid focusing on negatives

Negatives
- Not allowing balls to pass early
- Build innings within innings
- Footwork, lack of back-foot shots

Other
- Get quote to replace pool decking
- New golf clubs

*Taebok is a combination of yoga, pilates and kickboxing

May

27 Wednesday

Brisbane Airport

This morning we members of the Twenty20 squad assembled at Brisbane Airport (we'll be joined by the other Ashes squad guys in a few weeks). It's amazing to see how many of us there are these days. I can well remember when the Australian team would go away with nothing more than a physio, a team manager and a drinks waiter. And none of these blokes were exactly 'experts'. The team manager, for example, was generally a member of the Australian Cricket Board who the others wanted to get rid of for a few months (so they could make some sensible decisions). Nowadays we have a coach, assistant coach, physio, manager, fitness co-ordinator, masseuse, cricket analyst, fielding coach, bowling coach, batting coach, coaching coach and press officer.

No matter how excited we are about heading off on tour, there's always a tinge of sadness saying goodbye to loved ones. Being away from your family is an occupational hazard for any professional cricketer but I tell you, it doesn't get any easier. Three members of our squad are leaving behind partners expecting a child. (And there could be a fourth – he's just waiting on the results of a DNA test.)

I must say, packing for such a long tour is not easy. Even though it's summer over there we can expect a fair bit of rain and cold weather, so warm clothing will be required. On short tours, like over to New Zealand, you can travel pretty light but as we'll actually be in the UK for three months we have to take quite a bit of gear. Some of the boys are even packing a change of jocks.

Also joining us at the airport were members of my 2009 Supporters Tour Group. There's 18 of them; we had hoped for 20 but the last two discovered they couldn't leave the country under the terms of their bail conditions. They seem a nice bunch of blokes and I look forward to sharing with them the thrill of an Aussie Ashes campaign.

CAnews

May 2009

Cricket Australia – News

Well, it has been a busy few days in Coolum as the Australian cricket team assembled for its regular pre-Tour training camp. Also in attendance were our senior coaches and support staff who all took part in briefing sessions and a series of valuable discussions. This has been the first time that many senior Cricket Australia officials have had the opportunity to spend time with the current playing group and, as a result, several have tendered their immediate resignations. We wish them well. We also offer our best wishes to the Australian Twenty20 squad as they fly off to England for the ICC Cup. Amongst the team are several new faces making their international debuts. Meanwhile, we welcome back veteran players such as Brett Lee, Shane Watson and Warwick Todd who will all no doubt bolster the line-up with much needed maturity and experience.

May

28 Thursday

London

I must say our arrival at London's Heathrow Airport was fairly low-key. When we emerged from customs there was just a handful of waiting photographers and camera crews to welcome us. Some might argue that this has something to do with the lack of 'stars' such as Pigeon, Gilly and especially Warnie. There was certainly more excitement whenever you'd arrive somewhere with Warnie – he'd receive this massive cheer when he first walked through the arrivals lounge. After he'd done it for the fifth time the reaction would tend to die down a little.

The flight itself was uneventful, apart from a faulty smoke detector that kept going off whenever certain members of our middle order went into the dunny.

One person we were delighted to see waiting for us was Len Gough, our bus-driver-cum-baggage-master-cum-Mr Fixit. Len's job is to get us from venue to venue, handle our luggage, deal with ground authorities and, where necessary, bail us out of local lock-ups.

On a long tour such as this the team bus plays an important part. It's one of the few places where we players can truly relax out of the public gaze, unless of course we choose to press a part of our anatomy against one of the windows in which case it's a little harder to remain unnoticed. But this sort of behaviour rarely happens unless we have a big win or one of the boys is celebrating a birthday.

We were all given the day off to recover from the trip over (I believe a similar offer was made to the Qantas flight crew who looked after us), but there was one official duty – a visit to the Australian War Memorial near Hyde Park. Honouring our war heroes has become something of a tradition for Aussie squads, starting with a visit to Gallipoli in 2001, and then a trip to France back in 2005. As part of that visit I can vouch for the effect it had on everyone who travelled to Villers-Bretonneux where Australian troops fought during the First World War. I knew virtually nothing of this part of our history and most of the other guys admitted the same (in fact, Pigeon and Warnie had never even heard of France). But we all came away moved by the experience. Today's proceedings were no less sombre, with Punter laying a wreath at the foot of the memorial, just under the bit where it says 'officially opened by Prime Minister John Howard' (another of our fallen Aussies). Then Pup read from Laurence Binyon's oft-quoted poem 'For the Fallen'.

> *They shall not grow old, as we that are left grow old;*
> *Age shall not weary them, nor the years condemn.*
> *At the going down of the sun and in the morning*
> *We will remember them.*
> *Aussie Aussie Aussie, oi, oi, oi.*

It was certainly a quiet drive up to Birmingham. Whether this was due to the boys reflecting on those thousands of Australians who paid the ultimate sacrifice for our freedom, or because most of us were watching DVDs, it's hard to say. But when you think about the horrors that our diggers endured, it certainly puts our own petty problems into perspective.

May

29 Friday

Birmingham

We had a light training session this morning for which we were divided into groups: batsmen, quicks, spinners, keeper and Mike Hussey. We focused on specific T20 skills with a lot of fielding and throwing drills. The session was closely watched over, not just by Vinny and the support coaching staff but by our official bodyguards. Even though England is considered a 'safe' country, security at major sporting events such as the T20 World Cup is always a concern and we have been assigned a team from the Special Task Force. They are basically ex-British SAS officers who have failed to meet the stringent weight and/or fitness requirements so are now working in the private sector. After training, Punter faced his first official press conference. For the first time in my memory, Australia is not entering a tournament as favourite. And the fact is, we've only won 11 out of the 21 Twenty20 internationals played so far. Our last official match was in May when we took on Pakistan in Dubai and were beaten. I didn't play in this match due to a 'technical issue' with my choice of walk-on song; it seems the fuddy duddies at Cricket Australia deemed *Slap My Bitch Up* not 'family friendly'. All I was trying to do was inject a bit of modern musical flavour into the event. They should have heard my first choice.

Up until now Punter's been talking down our chances but today he started our war of words with England by suggesting that a half-fit Andy Flintoff won't be of much help during their Ashes campaign. Flintoff suffered a knee injury during the IPL. Meanwhile, Kevin Pietersen is battling an Achilles injury, also sustained during the IPL. Mind games like this are an important part of the lead-up to any series, but you've got to be careful. It's one thing to plant a few seeds of doubt in the enemy camp, but you don't want to say anything that might be used by the Poms as motivation. I was very careful about this when chatting to a local journo this afternoon.

An interesting interview with Pup appeared in the paper today in which he declared that he has 'no interest' in the captaincy and is determined to continue playing under Punter. You don't have to be a genius to see what's happening here; our vice-captain is clearly plotting his move into the top job. There's no way any player declares their 'full support' for the captain unless they're angling for a takeover. It's like coming out in the press and announcing you're 'happily married'. Whenever that happens you know things are looking grim on the home-front.

Our coach Vinny often comes up with interesting training drills, designed to really test us.
This morning's exercises were intended to sharpen reflexes and to mask the fact that he'd
left our bats and cricket balls back at the hotel.

Birmingham

THE **Daily Star**

www.thedailystar.co.uk

30p

Saturday, May 30, 2009

Poms a 'pack of girls'
Aussie batsman slams our team

Speaking after a team training session in Nottingham, senior Australian batsman Warwick Todd has questioned the talent, dedication, experience and sexual orientation of the entire England squad, with a withering verbal attack. Todd also took a swipe at British food, our weather and the late Queen Mother, whom he described as (cont. p.2)

I've pulled up well from yesterday's training session and this morning I decided to get up early and go for a run. Partly for fitness, and partly to keep clear of Punter for a few hours. I know Birmingham quite well as it was here that I first played county cricket as a fresh-faced 19-year-old. Talk about a tough apprenticeship! All I remember is being cold and wet for weeks on end. You'd stand in the outfield wearing thermal underwear and three jumpers and the wind would still cut through you. As the overseas 'import' I was by far the youngest member of the team. In fact, there were some really old codgers playing back then, some well into their sixties. During one match our vice-captain retired hurt, due to a sudden onset of gout.

I was sharing a flat with a friend of my brother's but it was still a half an hour drive away. Each night we'd train 'til late, I'd then have to drive home, grab a few hours kip and get up to start another part-time job in the morning. One evening I fell asleep at the wheel and managed to crash my car into a bus stop. The next morning I woke up to find four or five local media people gathered outside my flat wanting to talk with me. Little did I realise it at the time, but this was my first ever press conference!

Probably the only reason I survived that summer was thanks to the Barringtons, a wonderful local family who pretty much adopted me. Bronwyn and Mick Barrington made a point of looking after newly arrived Aussie cricketers and each night after training I would go round to their house for a roast and a pint or two. Bronwyn even used to do my washing and they'd lend me a few quid when I needed it to tide me over to my next pay day. I'll always appreciate how the Barringtons helped me get started as a cricketer, and taking them both to court was one of the hardest things I've ever had to do. But using my image without permission to promote their new bed and breakfast business (Todd Mews) was simply not acceptable and we had no choice but to take action.

England was really where my problems with alcohol started. I'd drunk beer before, but only in small glasses. You'd walk into an English pub and someone would put a glass the size of a bucket in front of you. I'd ask for 'half' and they'd say 'that is half'. Naturally you didn't want to be rude and, as I was always taught to finish what's on my plate, I'd have to drink it.

Tonight we received the bad news that we were expected to attend a civic function. Overseas tours are full of these, and the boys hate them, but we're expected to show up. This one featured the usual boring speeches and welcomes from local dignitaries. Just when we thought things were over, the Mayor got up to propose a toast, during which he rambled on about everything from England's chances of regaining the Ashes through to his plans for a new pedestrian overpass in the city centre. If it wasn't for the free drinks and half-decent food it would have been a hell of a long night.

May

31 Sunday

Birmingham

With just 24 hours to go until our first practice match everyone is in pretty good shape. The only real worry is Punter who had an injury scare during practice yesterday. He was picking up a ball in the nets when he was hit on the wrist by another cricket ball, struck by Michael Hussey. Luckily no serious damage was done to our skipper, which is more than can be said for Huss, who was chased off the field and forced to spend the remainder of the session hiding in a committee room. But both should be ready to take the field tomorrow. As a squad I believe we're really beginning to gel, although there are still a few issues yet to resolve. Nicknames is one. Dave Warner dropped a bombshell last night when he asked us to address him as 'Warnie'. He'd have to be f*#king kidding.

While much of our focus in recent months has been on the Ashes, we are taking the T20 tournament every bit as seriously. Like it or not, this high-octane form of the game is here to stay. From five-day Tests to one-day internationals, and now Twenty20, the game is getting faster, and this trend will only continue. There's word out that India are trialling a new 10-over version of the game involving two bowlers operating simultaneously from both ends. Okay, the purists might throw up their hands in horror, but if it keeps fans coming through the gates I've got no problem with it.

One side effect of the boom in T20 has been the invention of new bats, specifically made for the shortened form of the game. I've been working with my equipment sponsor on a new design that is thicker and heavier than most others. More importantly, it has a 97% sweet spot, so you can hit the ball harder and further no matter where it connects. Unfortunately, however, we've just received some bad news from the ICC that the 'Club' (as we've named our new prototype) does not comply with the rules of the game. On top of that, it has been placed on the UK's official register of prohibited imports (our only hope of making money back now is by selling it to private security firms or bikie gangs).

Made a quick trip down to London this afternoon to catch up with members of my supporters group. They were apparently a little pissed off about the flight over, being stuck down the back of the plane while we players were up front, so I've promised them a meet and greet with the entire team tomorrow. I didn't mention that the team in question was Bangladesh but, if their form so far is anything to go by, they'll be too pissed to realise.

Interesting news from the Middle East today: the Afghanistan President Hamid Karzai is giving the go-ahead for the creation of a national cricket board. If you ask me this is a good thing for the game, as the more new teams there are competing at international level the better. And it will be relief for the Pakis – finally a tour they can refuse to go on due to security concerns.

When it comes to rules governing bats my suggestion is simple: if you can lift it you can use it.

Calling the game

During my brief retirement from first-class cricket I was thrilled to be asked to do some commentary for Channel 9. And, even though it was only a few domestic one-day matches, I learnt an enormous amount. You don't spend hours in a tiny room with the likes of Tony Greig and Ian Chappell without picking up a few things. The importance of deodorant, for example. With television commentary, the key is to add something to the pictures. You can't just say 'Smith is bowling'. We can all see that. But if you say 'Smith is bowling poorly' then you're adding something to the coverage. You might then say 'no surprises there' which is humour. Or 'he's probably still hung-over from last night's binge' which is defamatory and quite possibly the reason I'm no longer part of the Channel 9 team.

Taking the cake

One of the fringe benefits of doing commentary for ABC Radio is the way listeners will often send in cakes and other treats for you to enjoy during a long day in the box. But you have to be a little careful. In November 2007 I was part of the Grandstand team providing special comments during the Brisbane Test when a fan from Mullumbimby sent in a tray of home-baked cookies. I have absolutely no recollection of the afternoon session, other than vague memories of Jim Maxwell playing air guitar and telling our statistician Laurel that he loved her.

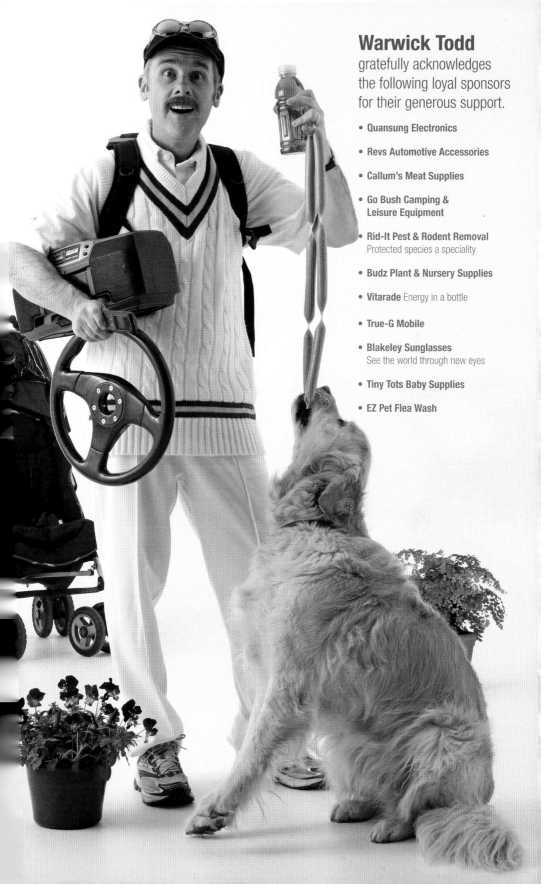

Warwick Todd
gratefully acknowledges
the following loyal sponsors
for their generous support.

- **Quansung Electronics**

- **Revs Automotive Accessories**

- **Callum's Meat Supplies**

- **Go Bush Camping &
  Leisure Equipment**

- **Rid-It Pest & Rodent Removal**
  Protected species a speciality

- **Budz Plant & Nursery Supplies**

- **Vitarade** Energy in a bottle

- **True-G Mobile**

- **Blakeley Sunglasses**
  See the world through new eyes

- **Tiny Tots Baby Supplies**

- **EZ Pet Flea Wash**

International cricketer Warwick Todd says:

"Don't let hair loss ruin your life. Make an appointment to speak with one of their qualified consultants now. And hit hair loss for six!"

After 1 week

After 2 weeks

After 3 weeks

After 1 month

No matter what the state of your scalp, Hair2Stay studios offer a range of options. They can replace, re-grow or simply re-carpet.

Nothing synthetic! All Hair2Stay products are made from REAL hair.

Hair2Stay consultants are all fully qualified and/or wear white coats.

Re-grow your own hair in our studios, or at home using our handy porta-packs.

You will see visible benefits within three months (two months in low light).

Dormant hair follicles can be stimulated with just a few thousand volts.

Our uniquely patented dollar-by-dollar® treatments allow you to regain your hair the way you lost it ... disturbingly.

Call Now! Our qualified hair-care consultants are standing by to cement your lack of self-confidence.

I have no trouble recommending the team at Hair2Stay for one simple reason – they're paying me to. Hair to stay? That's what I say!

Warwick Todd

Unfortunately my hair transplant failed to take, the result of overly tight batting helmets. But I still got paid for fronting the ad campaign.

WARWICK | FANS | MEDIA | FAQs | DOWNLOADS | SHOP | LINKS | SITE | CONTACT

INFORMATION | ITINERARY

Monday 15 June

Depart Australia flying Air Parnassus, via Jakarta (re-fuelling), Mumbai (change of air crew), Kuwait City (don't ask) and Heathrow.

Tuesday 16 June

Arrive London where you will be transferred to your hotel. Here you will stay in a quadruple share room for the next four nights on a bed or breakfast basis (not both). The rest of the day is at leisure.

Wednesday 17 June

The rest of the day is at leisure. In the evening re-live the excitement of the 2005 Ashes series with a DVD screening in the hotel function room (drinks at bar prices).

Thursday 18 June

This morning you will be transferred to the Oval to watch ground preparations for tomorrow's ICC World Twenty20 Semi-Final. Exclusive photo opportunity with curator. This evening enjoy the build-up for tomorrow's final in one of London's most authentic Aussie-themed bars.

Friday 19 June

Ball-by-ball descriptions of play on the big screen at the hotel.

Saturday 20 June

At leisure in London for sightseeing. You may wish to book a sightseeing tour with your hotel concierge. Alternatively, you can shop at Harrods or take a boat trip on the Thames. Or just stay at the hotel and have an argument with your wife about whose idea this trip was and why you didn't agree to that villa in Tuscany.

Sunday 21 June

ICC World Twenty20 England 2009 Final.

A Reserve tickets at the Oval where you can watch every ball of this historic match beamed in from Lords on the big screen.

Monday 22 June

This morning you will take the high-speed Eurostar train to Paris. On arrival you will be met by a Todd Tours representative who will direct you back to your seat for the return trip to London. Ooh lah lah!

You will be joined by your tour coach driver (and his friend Ken; they will both share a room with you). After the tour you will be dropped off at your hotel, or close to it (depending on the size of your tip).

London's famous Cricket Museum provides a fascinating glimpse into the origins of this great game. TOP LEFT: The first recorded tail-ender to face short-pitched bowling. TOP RIGHT: Deceptius, the Roman god of spin. ABOVE: The captains of Thebes and Phoenicia shake after the toss.

June

1 Monday

Australia v Bangladesh (Warm-up match)
Trent Bridge

Even though it's only a warm-up game, there's always something extra special about the first hit-out of a series. With quite a few of us pushing for a spot in the team it was decided to hold off announcing the line-up until the very last minute. But at breakfast this morning Punter finally said the words I'd been waiting to hear: 'Toddy, you're in.' Unfortunately they were followed by the words 'my way' (he wanted to get to the toaster). In the end the decision was made to rest me (information that might have been useful before I set the f*#king alarm clock) and give some of the younger blokes a go.

It's good to be back at Trent Bridge as I've had a lot of success here over the years. Although, my last visit wasn't exactly a day to remember. It was at this ground, of course, during a one-day international back in 2005 that Punter and I were both fined for reacting inappropriately after being dismissed. I then copped an additional penalty for reacting inappropriately after being fined. All up, an expensive day at the office.

Anyway, we won the toss and decided to bat. Watto was the star of the innings, belting 52 off 23 balls, ably supported by BJ (47 off 29) and Pup (35 off 18), as Australia reached an impressive total of 6/219. All eyes were on Bing when he ran in for his first over on English soil since ankle surgery and, to be honest, the big fella looked a little shaky. I wouldn't say 'average' (although I was thinking it) but certainly not the wild paceman of old. Bangladesh's openers Tamim Iqbal and Zunaed Siddique both punished him early on, belting 18 off his first over. Symmo was also expensive, going for 17 runs off his one and only over. But in the end we restricted them to 7/181, giving us an easy victory.

Being just a practice match there was no team song performed back in the rooms. In fact, with the T20 competition we have to win the entire series before it will be sung (it can, however, be hummed after a semi-final win). I, for one, can't wait.

We invited the Bangladesh boys to share a drink after the match but most of them are Muslims and therefore couldn't join us. And this was despite me making the effort to organise light beer, which was a little disappointing. Still.

Speaking of 'disappointing', there was news reported here today that former Australian coach John Buchanan has been contracted by English cricket authorities to help them with their preparations for the Ashes. I'm not overly worried about the effect of this – in fact, I'm happy to see the Poms drown in a sea of motivational notes and quotes from Chinese philosophers – but I think it does show great disloyalty. Someone who knows the inner workings of the Aussie squad should not be allowed to share this knowledge with outsiders. Now, I know some readers might bring up my brief coaching role with

the Namibian team in 2006 but I think that's different. For a start, I was only there for seven weeks before the deportation order took effect. And secondly, there was no way the Namibians were ever going to pose a threat at international level. Getting them to run round between witches hats and stay off the old whoopee weed was about all I could manage. And at no stage did I lift the lid on what makes the Aussie team tick.

There's no doubting that technology has changed the way we, and the umpires, view cricket. So far broadcasters have given us stump-cam, Hawk-Eye, Hot Spot and the Snickometer. Word is for the T20 tournament they're working on an ultra-sound camera that will be able to detect both edges and benign polyps from the boundary line.

June

2 Tuesday

Australia v New Zealand (Warm-up match)
The Oval

Well, the trip down to London for this warm-up game was more than worth it, with a seven-wicket win the return for our efforts. And, even though I didn't play a large part on the field, I was pleased just to be named in the line-up. Despite coming late to Twenty20 cricket, I feel I've adapted well to this form of the game. Sure, it's fast and furious, but the fundamentals of batting still remain the same. Footwork, timing, placement, soft hands. Then you slog like shit. Unfortunately, I didn't get the chance to cut loose, as New Zealand won the toss and elected to bat. They lost openers Brendon McCullum and Jesse Ryder each for no score and were lucky to reach 147. I was happy with my contribution in the field, really concentrating on what we call the 'one percenters'. Turning fours into threes, threes into twos, twos into ones, ones into dot balls and, if the batsman doesn't even look like attempting a run, then simply getting in his face and letting him know he's struggling. Hopefully my intensity in this area more or less made up for the catch I dropped (we call that a 'one hundred percenter'), a sharp edge from Guptill off Bing. While our strike bowler might still be a little way off his best in terms of bowling, the venomous glare he fired my way after grassing the chance and subsequent cold shoulder shows that he's well on the way back to reaching his old form. Australia reached 3/151 with four balls to spare, due largely to a 104-run stand between Punter and Pup. It was great to see them both in such fine form, although it would have been nice if they'd let a few of us other guys waiting in the shed have a bit of time in the middle. Still, I'll take a victory any day.

Exciting news tonight that Mitch has just announced his engagement to long-time girlfriend Jessica Bratich. Naturally we had a few drinks back at the hotel, and a few more when he told us the news. As a recent divorcee, I'm certainly not about to start giving Mitch marital advice, although I did warn him to check his schedule before agreeing to any wedding date. We all still remember Adam Voges' dilemma earlier this year when a call-up for the South African one-day series clashed with his own wedding. I was personally stunned at Kenny deciding to forego his place on the tour, when you think of the guys who'd give their left nut to make the Aussie squad. It's like those players you read about who insist on being at the birth of their kids. Given many of them weren't there at the conception, I really can't see the fuss.

D.I.V.O.R.C.E. – Toddy's Take

There's no doubting that balancing life as an international cricketer and a family man is not easy. Constant touring, time away from home, long lonely nights in hotel rooms with nothing but the mini-bar and a well-thumbed copy of *Wisden* for company. Now I'm not saying cricket was completely to blame for the break up of my marriage (I think history will show that Ros was pretty much the main culprit), but the many months away certainly didn't help.

I'm not going to use this book to bag Ros, or list all the ways she contributed to the end of our marriage. That would be unfair to her, and difficult to fit into the space available in a publication this size. Let's just leave it by saying the blame for our marriage breakdown was fifty-fifty. Half of it was her fault, the other half simply circumstances beyond anyone's control.

Naturally, when a relationship ends you go through a lot of inner doubt. You think, 'Could I have done more to make it work?' 'Was it my fault?' 'Should I have tried a little bit harder?' The answer is, of course, no, it was her fault.

We tried counselling but it didn't seem to help. All those expensive talk sessions seemed to do was give Ros an excuse for bringing up old issues. Like the fact that I *apparently* turned up drunk to the birth of our first child. What can I say? At least I turned up! I've played with blokes at state level who have missed their child being born because it clashed with a weights session.

So we ended up getting divorced. After announcing it to the press with the usual 'hope to stay good friends and please respect our privacy' line we both agreed to maintain a dignified silence, an undertaking that pretty much went out the window two weeks later when Ros agreed to take part in a *Today Tonight* re-enactment of our final days together.

June

3 Wednesday

London

As usual the English tabloids have been up to their same old lame tricks. London's *Sun* newspaper today published a doctored photo of Andrew 'Macca' McDonald looking like Ronald McDonald, complete with red wig and yellow jumpsuit. Honestly, the lengths these so-called journalists will go in order to unsettle us Aussies. I can still remember when they once bailed up struggling Australian captain Mark Taylor in the lobby of our team hotel and presented him with an over-sized bat. It was an awkward moment, embarrassing not just for Tubby, but also for me as I was one of the people who helped organise it.

With just three days left until our first official match, training has really stepped up a notch. I spent 45 minutes in the gym this morning. Admittedly most of that time was spent watching ESPN on one of the TVs in the aerobics room, but I feel that simply being surrounded by fitness equipment is often enough for a reasonable workout. Quite a few of the boys were keen to watch the first State of Origin match from back home and, as usual, the Queensland v New South Wales rivalry was pretty intense.

After lunch we all headed outside to the training facilities for some fielding drills. These consisted of having to catch a series of skied balls. Anyone who dropped one was forced to either do 20 push-ups or attend tomorrow's team meeting. We also practised sliding saves and hitting the wicket from side on before heading to the nets for some serious batting practice. I once read somewhere that the energy generated at a good net session would be the equivalent of that produced by a medium-sized nuclear power station running full bore for a week. There was certainly an intensity about our training today, with every bowler really bending his back and us batsmen testing out a variety of strokes. I'm working on a new shot for the T20 Championship; it's a reverse-reverse sweep, which I may actually register, once I can work out how to stop the bat flying out of my hands.

All training sessions are held under the watchful eye of our coach Vinny. There's no doubting it, he loves his cricket and is forever talking about it, analysing shots, discussing past performances, comparing different techniques and various batting styles. He's a great bloke to have as part of the squad, provided you don't get stuck next to him at dinner.

The reverse-reverse sweep still needs work. At this stage I'm more likely to be struck by my own bat than the ball. But it could well prove to be a match winner.

Tonight we all climbed into our best suits for the Professional Cricketers Association dinner at the Royal Garden Hotel in Kensington. This is yet another one of those tedious functions we're expected to attend on tour – an evening of old English codgers drinking whisky and banging on about the 'golden days' (of 2005). I tell you what, these are not exactly the boys' favourite ways to spend a night. We're often seated one to a table with people who are either cricket tragics or who don't know much about the game. In either case, they will want to speak to us and – what's more – expect us to speak back. Worse, we've been told no iPods.

June

4 Thursday

London

Talk about waking up to a bombshell! This morning we were informed that our team-mate Andrew Symonds had been sacked from the squad and was on his way back home. The official reason is that he had broken a number of team rules (as well as a hotel room window). There was also some sort of 'alcohol-related incident' that team management wouldn't go into, possibly for fear of offending one of our sponsors, but it must have been pretty serious. Personally I'm gutted, especially as I've always played something of a mentoring role with Roy. I was there with him that night in Cardiff, I helped organise the Darwin fishing trip that caused him to miss a team meeting, I was the one who dared him to go on radio and call Brendon McCullum 'a piece of s—t'. I know it's crazy, but I almost feel partly to blame. It's funny, I suspected something was up at training yesterday, and it wasn't just that the big Queenslander arrived late. It was also the fact he arrived in a wheelie bin. Anyway, our Leadership Group felt they had no choice but to ask him to fly home. I'm not sure what the future now holds for Symmo. His Cricket Australia contract expires at the end of this month, so at least he's got another three weeks to enjoy. The fact is, he's a truly gifted athlete, a powerful hitter and a wonderful team man. But he clearly has a problem with alcohol. His only choice would seem to be some serious counselling. Or taking up rugby league.

On a practical level, we are now down a key member and so training at The Oval today took on an even greater intensity. Vinny actually had his tracksuit on, so you could tell from the start things were serious. Annoyingly, training was cut short so we could all pose for the official team photo. You'd think that getting a dozen or so guys together in a group would be easy, but there are always unforeseen difficulties. For a start, seating can be an issue. Obviously Punter, Pup and senior team management get to sit up the front. But then it gets tricky. Do you go in order of matches played? Age? Strike rate? Ear size? Then there are guys who don't want, for sponsorship reasons, to be next to other guys. So managers often get involved and before you know it we're into a full-on s—t-fight. After about an hour or so of wrangling we were finally ready for the shot and final checks were done: faces clean, no unauthorised logos visible, everyone's old fella well and truly tucked out of sight. Snap. Done.

I simply cannot get my head around what makes someone like Roy behave the way he does.

Back at the hotel I received an angry call from members of my supporters tour group who were pissed off that I didn't show at last night's scheduled Drinks with Toddy event. They were being a little unreasonable, seeing as I had sent along a taped message of welcome and some signed team merchandise. They're also unhappy with their accommodation so I may be forced to find them a better youth hostel, preferably one with running water. A few people have questioned the wisdom of leading a supporters tour while still actually part of the Australian squad, suggesting it may be an over-commitment. But I'm confident that, with careful time management and a cap on the number of personal appearances I promise to make, it won't be a problem. (However, from now on I might consider checking into team hotels under a false name just to stop some of the more demanding members tracking me down.)

June

5   Friday

London

Early start today, with all the boys assembling for a scheduled team media session. This has been a feature of most tours for the past decade, a chance to take care of all pre-series media commitments in the one hit. Let's face it, on an average tour we players get hundreds of interview requests, from sports writers, radio broadcasters, TV stations and police officers, and to do them all would leave us virtually no time to train! The morning was spent with all of us sitting down individually and being asked our thoughts on the upcoming ICC series and our opponents. Cricket Australia will then spend the rest of the day dealing with any fallout from comments made by us during this session and issuing retractions, clarifications or – in extreme cases – unreserved apologies.

Shock news from the early rounds today – England was defeated by the Netherlands! Reminds me of the time we got done in a one-day international by Bangladesh – mind you, we were battling injuries and Symmo was pissed. The Poms must now beat the Pakis on Sunday to stay in the tournament. 'Clogs 1, Clots 0' said the headlines. England are naturally struggling to find excuses. Some players claim they were dazzled by the Dutch uniforms, the bright orange making it hard to pick up the ball. Wait 'til they meet the Irish.

High excitement today as a few wives and long-term girlfriends arrived at the team hotel (while a few other not-so-long-term girlfriends were snuck out a rear door). I know debate continues in the press back home as to whether or not our partners should be allowed on tour. And, while I'm all for family unity, I do recognise that having partners around can create some problems. Let's face it, the girls love to talk and sometimes a quite innocent incident can be witnessed by one of them and then misinterpreted. True story. On our last visit here in 2005 a certain player, let's just call him Batsman A, had his wife join him on the tour and they were coming back from a restaurant with another player, Batsman B, when they noticed a couple of young ladies emerge from the hotel room of a third player, Leg Spinner C. Well naturally Batsmen A and B knew to keep quiet but Batsman A's wife lost no time in jumping on the phone and letting all the other girls know about the incident. End result – awkwardness all round.

Women on tour – Toddy's Take

The question of whether wives and girlfriends should join us on tour is a vexed one. In the old days, of course, it simply didn't happen. Players farewelled their partners at the airport, often with little more than a handshake or an affectionate punch on the shoulder, and then headed off. And that's the way I suspect many of the guys would still  like it. Things really started to change under Tubby's captaincy when the ladies were allowed to join us mid-way through a tour. By the time Tugga took over, the girls were even allowed to talk to us (on non-match days) and join in some of the team social activities.

I'll be honest, I do have reservations. When we're on tour without the wives we tend to go out in big groups. All the boys will meet in the hotel bar for an unofficial bonding session over a few beers, before heading off as a group. But with the girls there this doesn't work so well. For a start, a lot of them drink wine, which can get confusing. And what about the blokes who don't have a partner? They can suddenly find themselves left out of social activities. Who can forget Shaun Tait on the '05 Ashes tour? As a relatively new member of the squad he was so isolated that at one stage he was forced to have dinner with our bus driver! Not fair on Sloony and not exactly good for team unity (although I believe the two of them became quite close and still stay in touch).

If you ask me, the obvious compromise is to start the tour without the ladies. Let us blokes focus on the task at hand, and bond as a team. Then the girls can come across towards the back end of the trip, say, around Day Four of the final Test.

June

6 Saturday

Australia v West Indies
The Oval

Whether it's Test cricket, one-day internationals or Twenty20, there's always a heightened level of excitement surrounding the first official match of a series. This is where all the training, planning, meetings and personal preparations pay off, where we get to showcase our skills as elite athletes on the world stage. Which makes today's loss even harder to understand. Of course, it's tempting in situations like this to blame others. Watto and Punter making ducks. Pup going for just two. Bing conceding 24 runs in an over. But that's not my style. Those blokes know who they are, they know what they did (or failed to do), cricket's a team game and we need to all take responsibility as a team for today's loss. The last thing I want to read is 'Todd's 37 off 15 balls was batting at its brilliant best, but he was sadly let down by lack of support at the other end'. It may be true, but it's not what I want to read. And let's not take anything away from the West Indies. They played quite well and – with the help of a few soft decisions and some sloppy fielding on our part – they thoroughly deserved their freak win.

It might look like Punter's annoyed at me but we're simply discussing fielding positions.
I'm proposing I move to second slip. He's proposing I get the f*#k back to long off.

We heard after play today that the West Indies have lodged an official complaint about racial abuse being levelled at them by Australian spectators. For the Windies to have complained, the taunts must have been pretty ugly and we've naturally agreed to co-operate with any investigation. As far as I'm concerned, the sooner these fools are identified and banned from attending matches the better for us all.

To his credit, Punter did not dwell on today's performance at our post-match team meeting. Both he and Vinny are smart enough to know that everyone realises how badly we performed without having someone stand at the front of the room banging a table. We're all adults and a far more mature approach is called for. So we just had a quick team meeting to cover some technical issues and then we were all sent to our rooms without dinner.

Power of the pen

Over the years the Aussie team has been lucky to have some gifted home-grown 'poets', fans with a gift for the gab who are often invited to address and inspire the squad before a big day's play. For this Twenty20 tournament long-time supporter and wordsmith Stuart Blake joined us and presented this ode to the team.

> *It's the boys from down under in their green and gold*
> *Who will never give up until victory they hold*
> *When the game's on the line and there to be won*
> *It's the boys from AUSTRALIA who will be number one.*
> *AUSTRALIA, AUSTRALIA, AUSTRALIA, AUSTRALIA you are the best*
> *No matter how hard, we never will rest*
> *AUSTRALIA, AUSTRALIA, AUSTRALIA, AUSTRALIA, AUSTRALIA*
> *AUSTRALIA AUSTRALIA AUSTRALIA …*

It was a pity we had to cut him short (as there were apparently another seven verses to go) but we had to get out on the ground. Blakey didn't take this well and soon after quit his position as unofficial Tour Poet. (We later heard he was writing for New Zealand.)

June

7 Sunday

Nottingham

Shit. Turns out the 'racist spectators' at yesterday's game were all members of my supporters group, just trying to, in their words, 'unsettle the darkies for us'. I've told them to lay low.

Heavy rain this morning caused the cancellation of our scheduled training session here at Nottingham; so, instead, we bunkered down for a team meeting on how we can best hope to defeat Sri Lanka in tomorrow's match. A few of the boys have managed to download some offensive Tamil expressions from the Internet that we might be able to use out in the middle – if any of us can learn how to pronounce them.

I told members of my supporters group to keep a low profile. Not sure the message got through.

This tournament marks the first time we've seen the Sri Lankan boys since that horrific attack on their team bus in Pakistan earlier this year. Like all sportsmen, I was shocked and saddened to hear of this incident. For terrorists to target hotels and schools is one thing, but to attack a visiting first-class cricket team is clearly crossing the line. Fortunately, none of the Sri Lankan players involved were killed and I'm told Pakistani police working on the case have narrowed their list of likely suspects down to just under four million. What it does mean for cricket, of course, is that no team is now prepared to tour Pakistan. Whether we'll ever tour there again remains unclear. Earlier this year Cricket Australia sent a security expert over to Islamabad to assess the situation but he hasn't been heard of in over six months.

Roy's replacement, Cameron White, arrived today to help bolster the squad, so naturally we shared a few drinks to welcome him on board. The papers over here are still full of stories about our 'disgraced Aussie' team-mate and his public drinking exploits. Talk about a beat up! From what I can tell, Roy simply enjoyed a few beers last week while watching the State of Origin match with our rugby league social committee. I guess the fact he was the only member of this committee has created a few issues for team authorities. Our skipper gave an interview yesterday in which he spoke of Roy's battle with alcohol and expressed the feeling that, for quite some time now, the Queensland all-rounder has 'not been in a good place'. You got that right Punter, he's been in the pub. Whatever we might say publicly, the fallout from Symmo's departure continues to be felt. According to inside sources, Cricket Australia chiefs back in Australia have just called a crisis meeting after receiving his hotel room mini-bar bill. Apparently the Reserve Bank may have to get involved.

There are a few days off next week and my manager has booked me on a pretty hectic schedule of meetings with sponsors, not to mention a few corporate engagements. I've just found out I'm doing a motivational speech on Tuesday for a group of British investment brokers. They want me to talk on the topic 'the importance of embracing change', which is great because I'll be able to use most of my old material.

June

8 Monday

Australia v Sri Lanka
Trent Bridge

Well, what can I say? Not one of our finest days on a sporting field. And we are now out of contention for the ICC Twenty20 World Cup, courtesy of a six-wicket loss to Sri Lanka. Our only hope for remaining in the competition would be for the Netherlands to beat Pakistan, New Zealand to forfeit to South Africa, the Sri Lanka v West Indies match getting rained out and the entire Irish team to test positive for a banned diuretic. Fingers crossed.

It's hard to say exactly what went wrong today. After losing the toss and being sent in, I guess none of us really managed to get on top of Sri Lanka's spin-bowling attack. A few of us got starts, but no one built on them. I fell for 16 after attempting what one ill-informed commentator called a 'rash sweep'. For god's sake, this is Twenty20 cricket, what do they expect? A few overs worth of bat-pad nudges while I just 'get my eye in'? In this form of the game you've got to go out there all guns blazing, especially when most of your team-mates have failed to get a start. I'm not blaming anyone personally, and blokes like Huss or Lloyd shouldn't have to shoulder all of the responsibility for today's loss. The fact is, none of us were able to get on top of the Sri Lankan's spin attack.

It was Punter, as usual, who summed things up, telling the team, 'Okay, it's time we re-group and set our focus on winning the Ashes.' The fact he said this just before going out to bat perhaps summed up our general lack of confidence. We really didn't believe in ourselves.

By the time we got back to the hotel I think the reality of what happened today had begun to sink in. Brute, Vinny and Punter called an emergency team meeting where they talked about our performance and the fact that, yet again, we've failed to make an impact on the world Twenty20 scene. Punter then got up and spoke about his genuine disappointment at our shock loss. Our skipper plays the game hard and with all his heart, and to see him choked up like this in front of the boys was pretty confronting. He was genuinely distressed about being bundled out and after he finished speaking there was complete silence in the room. Vinny then said, 'Does anyone have any questions?' Sidds asked, 'Are we still having Italian tonight?' Meeting over.

A little later we gathered for a few drinks at the hotel bar but, I have to tell you, those beers felt pretty flat. However, in the interests of team bonding, we forced ourselves to enjoy a big night.

I'm not exactly sure what the Sri Lankans said to me as I walked off but I've got a strong suspicion it may have been racist. I plan to be offended just as soon as I get an accurate translation.

Fair pay – Toddy's Take

Good news from home on the contract front. The Australian Cricketers' Association has just struck a new pay deal with Cricket Australia. Under the terms of the agreement we have re-committed to upholding the spirit of the game, both on field and off. Cricket Australia have, in turn, agreed to raise match payments and ban water-boarding from their player counselling sessions.

It's amazing what agreeing to a photo with the owner can do. TOP: Discount fridge? Thanks very much. ABOVE: Who pays for a feed these days?

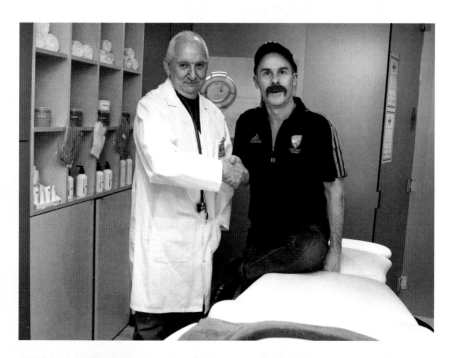

TOP: Another cost-free colonoscopy! ABOVE: Grandpa's funeral – dignified and dirt cheap.

In Profile

Warwick Todd, Australian cricketer

My earliest memory is:
Playing cricket in the backyard with my brother Damien.

My first love was:
My Gray Nicholls triple scoop bat.

My mother and father always told me:
Get in behind the line of the ball.

My last meal would be:
It depends whether or not it's the night before a match because when I'm playing I like to avoid carbs.

The things I hate most are:
Poverty, cruelty to animals (except cats, I hate them) and prejudice. I also hate damp towels when you get out of the shower.

My happiest moment was:
The day I got married. And even though it was pretty much downhill from then on I still think back to that special day and the few small bits I can remember before I passed out in the limo.

The hardest thing I've ever done is:
Learn to not play across myself.

Favourite place to be on holiday:
On the balcony of a Gold Coast apartment block watching as you cast shadows on the beach below.

Three people you'd invite to a dinner party:
I'd like to say Sir Donald Bradman but I've heard he could be a bit of a grump, so how about Nelson Mandela, Mahatma Gandalf and Suzie Wilkes.

The last time I cried:
Last year, watching a Pura Cup highlights package.

My greatest regrets would be:
Getting knocked out of the 2009 Twenty20 competition, falling three runs short of a double ton in India and letting the builder talk me into evaporative cooling. And Dad dying.

Nottingham

As usual after a big match we started the day with a recovery session, which this morning involved several Beroccas and a sleep-in. I'll be honest, there's something of a flat feeling amongst the boys right now. We had planned on spending the day with net sessions and Super 8 strategy meetings. Instead we're in BJ's room playing cards. And having to face up to the English newspapers, with their pathetic headlines like 'See ya shielas!' Or 'What do you call an Aussie at a Twenty20 match? A spectator!'

Of course, it's not just the local papers who are having a crack about yesterday's match and the reason we lost. One Australian cricket writer (i.e. a failed district player turned bitter hack) claimed it was because our squad is too old. Apparently only two of us are under the age of 27. So? We're not over here to tape an episode of *Home and F#*king Away*. Another journo genius has queried our reliance on pace, rather than spin. I'm telling you, when bowlers like Bing and Mitch are on song, no team can stop them. A third article, in the *Herald Sun*, questioned Punter's leadership, and his 'obvious inability to grasp the fundamentals of T20 cricket'. This one was so laughable that I just had to leave a copy under his hotel room door.

To add insult to injury, we've been fined for our slow over rates in yesterday's match, 5% for us and 10% for Punter. And on top of that I've received a 'please explain' from Cricket Australia over a joke I made a few days ago on English TV. I was a guest on some show called *Richard and Judy* (to be honest, I couldn't work out who was who) and all I said was 'What do you get when you cross a Paki with a Sri Lankan? A car thief who can't drive!' Apparently it's been deemed racist, despite the fact I didn't say which one was the thief (the Paki).

The key now is that we put all this behind us and make the most of the next two weeks. Word from home is that Cricket Australia are keen to organise some additional practice matches for us in the lead-up to the Ashes series. My biggest worry is what to do with my supporters group. They were expecting front-row seats at Australia's first Super 8 match but, at this stage, the best I can offer them is a 10% discount at Madame Tussaud's. Thank god we're heading to Leicester – at least I'll be out of reach.

June

10 Wednesday

Leicester

This Australian team is full of men with courage, commitment and a never-say-die, no-surrender attitude. If we're down, it's never for long.

After a light breakfast it was down to the ground for a lengthy net session. I did some work with our strength and conditioning coach (Stuart Karppinen) and a bowling machine (Peter Siddle), focusing on my head position and balance at the crease. After our net session, Vinny assembled us for a fielding drill involving a series of coloured plastic cones, each one representing a different skill: long flat throws, short shots at the wicket, deep catches. Depending on what cone you were closest to and how far away from the ball you were, you then executed the appropriate return before moving on to the next station. As an exercise, it was typical of our coach – inventive, challenging and different. Unfortunately, due to the amount of time it took him to explain the rules, we ran out of light and had to stop just a few minutes in.

Stretching is an important part of any training session. It's also a good chance to catch up with the news from home.

Unbelievable! I was accused today of revealing 'team tactics' via my Twitter alerts.

Tonight's team meeting was a lengthy one, but also, I think, the most productive of the tour so far. Led by Punter, BJ and Vinny, we kicked around what had gone wrong so far and how we can put it right. Everyone was invited to have their say and in the end we reached the following conclusions:

ON THE GROUND – get there early, get out on the field and take control, everyone to learn words of national anthem.
DISCIPLINE AND ATTITUDE – it's no good having outstanding skill levels if these levels are not executed to a similar level or beyond in skilful and excellent execution (I may have not got this totally right).
DO THE BASICS – building partnerships, at least one player making a big score, building pressure in the field, positive body language (slip cordon to all be chewing gum, don't just leave it to Punter).

This evening a few of the squad – myself, Huss, Bing, BJ – went out for dinner at an Indian restaurant close to our team hotel. This sort of informal socialising is important on a long tour and a good way for the squad to really bond, especially the newer players. In hindsight we should perhaps have invited a few of them, but somehow no one got round to it.

June

11 Thursday

Leicester

It's been announced that we will not be playing any additional matches in the next fortnight, partly because there's only 10 of us players still here. Also, Vinny wants us to spend more time in the nets, working on our form and stamina. As I said to one journo this morning, 'Our bowlers, in particular, really need to get their rhythm and line back into Test mode.' Practice today had an added air of excitement because it was our first hit-out with red balls and white pads since the South African tour. We've all got rid of the coloured clothing and equipment used during the Twenty20 series, which makes our kit-bags a lot lighter. Of course, this official tour gear is highly sought after and a lot of players get together with local charities where it can be used for fundraising. I sold one of my shirts to Oxfam for £75.

A formal dinner was scheduled tonight with several of Cricket Australia's key sponsors. These are important events and a lot of planning goes into the seating arrangements. Representatives from our principal sponsors such as VB or the Commonwealth Bank get to share a table with Punter or other senior players. Then there's people from companies like Ford or KFC who are known as 'official partners' – they're seated with our lesser known squad members. Finally, you've got minor supporters like Cadbury Schweppes who generally find themselves down the back with one of our skills coaches or reserve keeper. These events can be pretty tedious, trying to make conversation with some account manager from Milo. Luckily I ended up next to some bloke from Johnnie Walker so we had a fair bit in common.

The latest Queen's Birthday Honours were announced today and it's the usual collection of politicians, doctors, soldiers and soon-to-be-disgraced business leaders. Disappointingly I've been overlooked again, given the number of community initiatives that I've lent my name to over the years. I'm the Patron, Public Face or Ambassador of diseases I can't even pronounce, but does anyone care? Not that you do these things because you're after a pat on the back, but an Order of Australia would be a nice little square up. It's the tall poppy syndrome. No matter how much you put in, there's always knockers out there looking to find fault. Like my removal as spokesperson for Skin Smart Australia. Rather than focus on the five years I spent promoting sun safety around the country, they point to *one* series of ads I make for Bronze-World tanning salons in Melbourne and suddenly I'm damaged goods.

Charity begins at home

As a high-profile Australian sportsman I have always felt it important that I give of myself, which is why I established the Warwick Todd Foundation. It's a grassroots charity that raises money for a whole range of worthy causes, from youth homelessness to diseases such as sleep apnoea and that one where you dribble a lot. But it hasn't all been smooth sailing. In its early years the Foundation was plagued by staffing issues. After our first CEO was jailed for embezzlement I decided 'that's it, no more family members involved in managerial positions' and since then we've managed to grow steadily.

Last year we held a special night in Sydney, called Cricket Cares, designed to show how the cricket community – players, wives, officials – care about the underprivileged. Disappointingly, only about 70 people showed, mainly Cricket Australia office staff looking for a free feed, and the event could best  be considered a moderate failure. However, the next function, a charity ball, was more successful with 600 guests treated to some top-class entertainment from Australian music stars including Human Nature, Colette, the New Original Seekers and Jimmy Barnes (who sent a taped message). There were also auctions of sporting memorabilia, with a pair of my underpants worn on Day 1 of the 2005 Edgbaston Test generating quite a bit of interest; they were eventually snapped up by two men in bio-hazard suits who must have been acting for a third party.

June

12 Friday

Leicester

None of the bowlers are talking to me. They're apparently pissed off that I took a 'swipe' at them in the papers today. Talk about a beat-up. I never once used the phrase 'hopelessly inaccurate' or if I did it was in passing but that didn't stop the journo chucking it in a dozen times.

I'll be lying if I didn't say there was a bit of a flat feeling today as the first of the Super 8 matches got underway. I managed to call in a few favours and got my supporters group tickets to Ireland v Sri Lanka tomorrow. As it turns out, we've lost a few members of the group. One has been forced to return home after his wife discovered he was not really on a 'business trip'. I'm not exactly sure what tipped her off, perhaps the fact that he's been unemployed for the past three years. Another two have been detained by police for questioning after apparently attempting to hijack a London bus. They want me to organise a lawyer for them but I've pointed out that, under the terms of the trip, 'drinks, tips and emergency legal expenses are not covered'. Despite being out of the tournament we're trying to remain focused on the positives. The main one being, of course, that while England are still caught up in the shortened form of the game we are able to use the extra time to hone our Test playing skills. Actually, that's the only one. I spent the afternoon playing golf with a few of the boys. Nothing too competitive, although we did have a small wager on the result, just to keep things interesting.

Another official function tonight, a sort of stuffy dinner attended by several hundred paying guests. As usual we players were split up, one to a table, and spent the evening answering questions and signing autographs. Not my favourite way to spend time but we are all aware that, as ambassadors for Australia and Australian cricket, it's our responsibility to not only attend but to also create a favourable impression. Which makes it even harder to understand why BJ and Watto started the food fight. At least it cut short a few of the speeches.

Not surprisingly the West Indies defeated India, while Sri Lanka knocked off Pakistan. If we're barracking for anyone, it's the Sri Lankans. We Australian cricketers have a strong connection to Sri Lanka. In 2004 many of us visited to assist in repairing houses and schools damaged by the tsunami. We went back again in 2005 to assist in repairing the hotel room damaged by that earlier visit.

Tonight's function featured as guest speaker some ex-county coach who spoke about his personal battle with bi-polar disease. It was an emotional speech and, in hindsight, I felt bad about starting the slow hand-clap but he was going on a bit and we had to get out of there somehow.

June

13 Saturday

Still in f#*king Leicester

After a punishing fielding and fitness session yesterday, we were given the day off to explore the 'many delights' of Leicester. Half an hour later and we were back at the hotel.

Most of the boys then headed for the golf course or the local races but I decided to catch up on a couple of those tasks I've been putting off for the past few weeks. The first was a shower, then I got busy updating my website WarwickTodd.net. It's a great way for me to stay in touch with my fan base and I enjoy the online Q&A sessions.

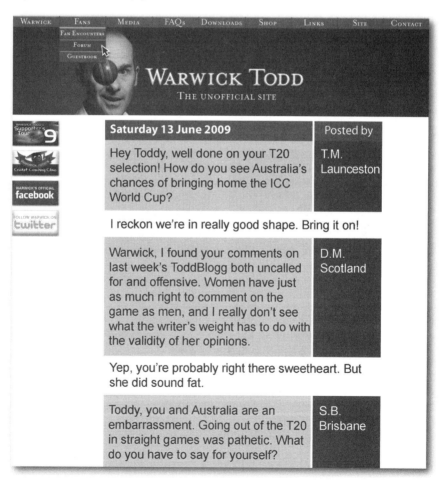

WARWICK   FANS   MEDIA   FAQs   DOWNLOADS   SHOP   LINKS   SITE   CONTACT
FAN ENCOUNTERS
FORUM
GUESTBOOK

WARWICK TODD
THE UNOFFICIAL SITE

Saturday 13 June 2009	Posted by
Hey Toddy, well done on your T20 selection! How do you see Australia's chances of bringing home the ICC World Cup?	T.M. Launceston

I reckon we're in really good shape. Bring it on!

Warwick, I found your comments on last week's ToddBlogg both uncalled for and offensive. Women have just as much right to comment on the game as men, and I really don't see what the writer's weight has to do with the validity of her opinions.	D.M. Scotland

Yep, you're probably right there sweetheart. But she did sound fat.

Toddy, you and Australia are an embarrassment. Going out of the T20 in straight games was pathetic. What do you have to say for yourself?	S.B. Brisbane

Listen mate, it's dickheads like you who give cricket fans a bad name. The boys and I put in 100%, we were simply beaten by luckier teams.

Mr Todd, we have taken the opportunity of contacting you via this site as you don't appear willing to answer your phone or regular mail address. Your account with our store is currently 90 days overdue and unless payment is received by the end of this week we shall be forced to initiate legal proceedings.	David Tzalt, Customer Credit Officer, Hobbes Electrical Superstores

(This forum is for genuine cricket-related questions only – Moderator)

How do you feel about your inability to beat India in India?	D.P. Panel, Mumbai

How do you feel about being a dickhead? Listen buddy, we'll start winning when you guys stop ball tampering.

An apology from WarwickTodd.net to Younus Khan

Last week an offensive comment regarding Younus Khan briefly appeared on this website. WarwickTodd.net immediately removed the comment and instigated an investigation into the circumstances under which it was published. It appears that the moderator responsible for the online discussion forum inadvertently uploaded part of a private Internet conversation onto the site. As soon as he realised the error he took steps to remove it, but the publication process meant that it was live for approximately 65 seconds. WarwickTodd.net deeply regrets the error and apologises to Younus Khan, his family and hairdresser for any distress the comment caused.

June

14 Sunday

Leicester

This morning a bunch of us met at the hotel pool for a few laps of walking – forwards, backwards, side to side and lunges. Following this we did some leg swings against the edge of the pool, by which time quite a crowd of spectators had gathered and we were asked to put on bathers.

Our bowlers have spent the past few days practising how to get swing from the Duke cricket balls that we will be using during the Ashes series, rather than our usual Kookaburra pills. A key to getting swing is keeping one side shiny while the other side gets roughed up, and each of our bowlers was given a ball last week and told to look after it, prompting Mitch to comment at dinner, 'We've been looking at each other's balls.' Or, at least, that's what we hoped he was talking about. Our bowlers work closely with coach Troy Cooley, the man who helped England's pace attack defeat us here four years ago. Cools has been concentrating mainly on their line and length and, by the start of the first Test, he hopes to have all our quicks swinging the ball both ways through the air. After that he'll be working on basic social skills and getting them to use cutlery.

Another good hit-out in the nets for me this afternoon, just tuning up a few elements. The adjustment between Twenty20 and first-class cricket is largely mental, but you do also have to remove certain shots from your repertoire, such as anything involving just the one hand. This morning we mainly worked on footwork and timing, the two fundamentals for any batsman. Our bowlers were coming in at pretty close to top speed. Personally, I like this in a net session, having blokes like Bing, Sidds or Mitch charging in. I know I'll cop a few bruised fingers but it's worth it.

Annoying news from my manager Neville back home. The f#*king graphic designers have stuffed up the ad for my charity cricket event in October. It was supposed to be WARWICK TODD'S HAVE A CRACK!, a one-day tournament designed to promote community health by encouraging people to give cricket a go. Turns out they've lost the apostrophe, meaning that several hundred VIPs and media have just been invited to something called the WARWICK TODD SHAVE A CRACK! day. What's that supposed to encourage? (Interestingly though, we have apparently had quite a bit of interest in the event.)

As a rule we try and avoid letting our fast bowlers spend too much time together unsupervised as it only leads to problems. This morning at training I overheard Watto, Hilfy and Sidds discussing plans to form their own leadership group. Meanwhile Bing, Mitch and Sarfraz had started a competition to see who could be the first to dislocate their own shoulder.

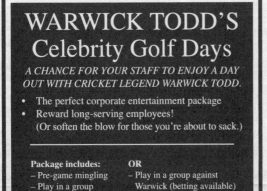

WARWICK TODD'S
Celebrity Golf Days

A CHANCE FOR YOUR STAFF TO ENJOY A DAY OUT WITH CRICKET LEGEND WARWICK TODD.

- The perfect corporate entertainment package
- Reward long-serving employees!
  (Or soften the blow for those you're about to sack.)

Package includes: **OR**
– Pre-game mingling   – Play in a group against
– Play in a group   Warwick (betting available)
  with Warwick   – Lunch and souvenir photo

My corporate golf days continue to be popular with the general public, despite some negative publicity after one group complained that I left after the first two holes. There's no pleasing some people.

June

15 Monday

Please get us out of Leicester

Up early for a breakfast speaking engagement. It's been organised by one of my sponsors and my job is to mingle with the guests, sign a few hundred autographs and then make a short speech explaining how my batting average has been directly helped by the use of their garden furniture. After this I took part in a short question and answer session with the audience, followed by a question and answer session with the local police. (It appears that a few works of art have gone missing from the hotel's foyer.)

I must say, the facilities at Grace Road are regarded as the best in England and it seems that just about every club and county side here in Leicestershire is offering to help us with training. We had a net session this morning at which some cocky little upstart from the under-17 squad really worked us over with a barrage of short stuff. He hit Bing on the finger, resulting in some rather nasty bruising (to both Bing and then the kid).

After batting practice we moved onto the oval to work with Youngie on our fielding. There were targets of different colours set up; green for short sharp throws, yellow for longer lobs and black ones that – I discovered after spearing a few returns in – were sprinklers. Then we did some running and fitness work with Stuey who has brought a new toy with him, a small parachute. The aim of this is to add resistance while running, and to make it harder for blokes to hide.

Back at the hotel I realised that I'm running perilously low on clean clothes. We've been away now for several weeks and I haven't done any actual washing, although I've been 'air-cleaning' a bit of gear by hanging it over the back of chairs. It reminds me of when I used to room with a certain former Australian skipper, let's just call him 'Steve', who had an interesting way of testing his clothes to see if they were wearable. He'd pick up an item from the floor and give it the 'sniff test'. One sniff and it was clean. Two sniffs meant it needed washing. Three sniffs and it was time to ask for a new room.

Former fast bowler Geoff Lawson wrote an article in the Australian press today questioning the wisdom of selecting Brett Lee for the current tour. It seems Henry thinks Bing is well past his best and highly unlikely to take many wickets. I made a copy for Bing who told me that he wanted to stay focused and wasn't interested in reading 'crap from home', which I thought was a bit disappointing, especially as I'd taken time to mark all the really negative bits for him with a highlighter pen.

Our team manager, Brute, organised a get-together this evening to thank all those who have been involved with us here in Leicester and to allow them to bring anything they would like to have signed. Which in my case turned out to be mainly bills from the hotel mini-bar, restaurant and cocktail lounge. Brute and Punter then made the usual speeches, thanking everyone for their hospitality and apologising for the damage to the lobby carpets.

Keeping clothes clean and dry on tour is a constant battle. I opt for the 'air wash' method; you just hang your gear up and hope the sweat or other stains will simply blow out in the breeze.

Selling out – Toddy's Take

These days most cricketers make as much if not more than
their Cricket Australia salary through personal endorsements.
Sponsorship is a wonderful thing as long as we always remember
that the good of the game comes first. Some young players want
big dollars before they've really proved themselves on the field. It
might sound hard to believe, but I played 17 Tests before I even
began to pretend I drank Milo. And it was two years into my one-day
international career before Sorbent 2-ply became a major part
of my life. The fact is, I prefer to endorse products I actually use.
Hence, I've never done an ad for multi-vitamins, organic mulch or
toilet cleaners. Let's face it, if people see Warwick Todd banging
on about some company he clearly knows nothing about then
there's a very real danger that they could lose respect for me.

I will not endorse anything. No matter what sort of money is being offered, if I feel a product is poorly made, over-priced or contains visible traces of an endangered animal species, then it will not receive the Todd tick of approval. As for any pharmaceutical item involving 'nasal delivery technology' all I can say is 'never again'.

I also take my responsibility to the community very seriously. For example, I recently refused to do a series of TV ads for pre-mixed alcoholic beverages until the agency *guaranteed* that the words 'drink responsibly' would be flashed up on the screen for at least a few seconds at the end.

As a rule, I try to go with companies that fit my image. For a lot of young kids out there, Warwick Todd is more than just a gifted cricketer. He's an icon. And I get pretty pissed off when I hear disgruntled ex-players criticising us for earning money from sponsors, suggesting that we no longer play for the love of the game. Every bloke I've ever shared an Australian dressing room with is 100% committed to the game; 120% if you factor in management and agent fees. Besides, let's not forget the work that goes into shooting an ad. To stand in some windowless TV studio holding a bat for hours on end while repeating the phrase 'Hit benign prostate enlargement for six!' over and over can really take it out of you.

No matter how careful you are, sometimes sponsorship deals can turn sour. It's one thing to appear in a few TV ads and maybe show up at a store opening or two. But when the owners start making unreasonable demands (such as wanting you to actually use their products) that's when things can go wrong.

Apart from direct endorsements I am also the 'ambassador' or 'public face' of several large companies. For example, I have a quiet deal with a Melbourne casino complex that involves handing over prize cheques to big winners and encouraging newly bankrupt gamblers to keep quiet.

June

16 Tuesday

London

After a recovery session at the gym we checked out and boarded the bus for the trip down to London where Test-only players Phillip Hughes (Boof), Simon Katich (Katto), Stuart Clark (Sarfraz), Marcus North (Snorks), Andrew McDonald (Ronnie) and Graham Manou (Choco) have arrived this morning. By the time the entire 15-man touring party gathered in our Kensington hotel there was quite a media contingent eager to speak with us all. It's funny watching some of the new, younger guys; they're all so keen to get into the nets or the gym. As a veteran of several Ashes campaigns, my advice is to not rush, take things slowly. I generally like to start long tours with a haircut.

Exciting news regarding my supporters group – they've been placed in quarantine after one of the remaining members developed symptoms of swine flu! Looks like I'm off the hook, at least until the test results come back.

Did an interview this morning with a local newspaper journo who mentioned to me that I needed just another 215 runs to reach 10,000 runs in Test cricket. It's unbelievable how obsessed some people get – I had no idea this milestone was looming. I'm simply not one of those players who gets hung up on statistics. To be honest, I couldn't tell you which player scored the fastest one-day 50 at the WACA*, or who was the first left-handed batsman to make consecutive centuries in his fourth Test** or who holds the record for second slip catches on the subcontinent.*** Sure, whoever it was must have been good. But the only innings that matters is my next one. And that's what I'm focusing on right now.

Interesting news from yesterday's Pakistan v Ireland clash. The Pakis have complained about the umpires' insistence on examining the ball between every over, saying it might have made them look like ball tamperers. Might? The Pakis are world champions when it comes to this stuff. Lifting the seam, scraping the surface, rubbing Tiger Balm into the leather. Seriously, you shake hands with a Paki bowler and come away with half your skin missing. I reckon the umpires should have been checking the ball between each delivery. (Not that I'd say something like this publicly!)

* Me
** Me again
*** W. Todd

Look, I'm all for visiting sick kids in hospital, but if they're not going to at least pretend to be interested in the history of this great game then you honestly have to ask yourself what's the point.

I work with a range of community groups, including the Australian Jewish Cricket Club, who I coached for several months. They're not a bad team and we could have made the finals last year if they'd been prepared to put in a little more effort, like showing up on a Saturday.

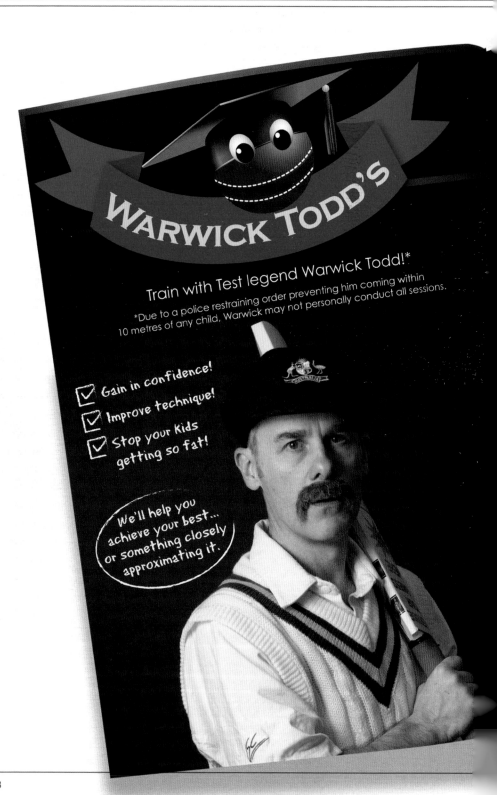

Cricket Coaching Clinic

Warwick Todd's Cricket Coaching Clinic opened in 2004, closing the following year for health and safety reasons before re-opening in '06. Since then it's gone on to become bigger, better and more expensive.

Catering for all levels:

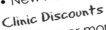

Non-smokers welcome!

- Beginners
- Intermediate
- Experienced
- Girls
- New Australians (by appointment)

Clinic Discounts

Book two or more places together and save on stamps!
Fully supervised, safe camp policies, kid friendly, drinks at bar prices.

Testimonials

I just wanted to say my son James attended your camp last week and since coming back he has not said one word. Thank-you!
– J.T.

I just wanted to say 'good on ya' Toddy' for helping our champions of tomorrow realize their inadequacies today.
– M.N.

My son Mitchell attended your clinic yesterday. Where is he?
– F.P.

*New!
Hard ball net practice – where fun meets fear.*

Cricket Australia wish to make it clear that they are not in any way associated with this coaching clinic.

Dancing daze!

Doing Channel 7's Dancing with the Stars was a truly wonderful experience. I felt I grew, as both a dancer and a person, going on an amazing and truly inspirational journey. Sure, being eliminated in round one came as something of a blow, but I don't regret a minute of it. And I'm sure I would have gone further had my instructor Rose not been badly injured during the fox trot. We're still not exactly sure what happened, I think she may have foxed when I trotted. Either that, or I took too big a delivery stride.

Cricket Australia's Perspective
by James Sutherland, CEO, Cricket Australia

All members of the Australian cricket squad have committed to abiding by the Spirit of Cricket agreement drawn up in 2003. Unfortunately, what happened at the Sydney Cricket Ground in January 2008 was a clear departure from that Code. During *says who?* the first innings Australian batsman Warwick Todd was reported for uttering an offensive and racist obscenity in the direction of Indian bowler Harbhajan Singh. This comment was clearly heard by Mr Singh, his captain, both umpires and – thanks to microphones placed in the stumps – television viewers around the country. A verbal altercation between Messrs Todd and Singh *How is that my fault?* then ensued, during which further equally offensive comments were made regarding the latter's parentage, sexuality, intelligence and dietary preferences. There were even remarks made about Mr *What, we're not allowed to talk now?* Singh's turban, including a suggestion that he could be concealing explosives within it. *I was having a laugh*

At the conclusion of play a hearing was convened during which *More like a witch hunt* Warwick Todd was formally charged with a Level 3.3 offence – offensive and insulting language amounting to racism. Mr Todd's argument that the charge should be downgraded to a Level 2.8 charge (offensive abuse not amounting to racism) on the grounds that 'evidence from Indians can never be trusted' was understandably dismissed by the adjudication panel.

As a mark of how seriously Cricket Australia regarded this incident, Warwick Todd was fined 100% of his match earning and suspended from the next three One Day Internationals. He was also ordered to apologise personally to Mr Singh, and to return his turban.

June

17 Wednesday

London

Apparently I did. No one told me that there were a couple of English journos in the bar last night, virtually taking notes during our *private* conversations. Honestly, what's the world coming to when you can't make lighthearted racial slurs without having them thrown back in your face.

After breakfast this morning Punter and Vinny sat down with each of the newly arrived players to make sure they knew what was expected of them behaviour-wise. We've got a big couple of weeks ahead of us and there's always a lot of media scrutiny on Aussie squads so it's important nothing goes wrong on or off the field. To help with this, each member of the playing group was assigned a 'buddy' who hopefully can help them stay on the straight and narrow. My original buddy was Roy but now that he's gone home we'll go back to the tactic used in 2005 and I'll be fitted with an electronic bracelet.

As we couldn't use Lords or The Oval (both still being tied up by the T20 finals) we were forced to make the 97 km trip to Canterbury for training. This was not such a bad thing, as it gave the boys time to bond. The new arrivals were actually given the option of a rest day to get over their jet lag, but most were keen to come along with the rest of us.

Australian Team Bus

The following activities are <u>not</u> permitted:

* Smoking
* Spitting
* Golf
* Attempting to deliberately distract driver
* The consumption of alcoholic beverages
* Exposing any part of body outside
windows (without captain's permission)

Back at the hotel it was a quiet evening, with most of us playing pool, table tennis or darts. A few of the boys got bored and tried combining table tennis with darts but this activity had to be abandoned due to complaints and blood loss.

Dinner tonight became a sort of unofficial 'welcome' to the new members of our squad. Naturally a few tall stories were told and several drinks enjoyed. I had promised myself an early night but a small group of us kicked on at a London nightclub and, by the time I made it back to the team hotel, I realised to my shock that it was 5.30 am. On Friday.

Junior talent – Toddy's Take

I have serious reservations about the sort of restrictions placed on kids at junior level these days. Quite often you'll see a young bowler send down four or five excellent overs, only to be taken off in order to 'give someone else a turn'. Similarly, a batsman might be well on his way to a half or even full century and they're forced to 'retire' so that some over-weight no-hoper with an anxiety disorder gets his turn at the crease. These gifted kids are our future champions and they need to be given a taste of what it's like to truly grind an opposition into the dirt while their less talented team-mates watch and applaud. Cricket is not about giving everyone 'a go'. It's about letting the best be the best. True story. A friend of mine has a son who goes to a school where they don't award places during athletic carnivals. No 'first', 'second' or 'third'. Everyone simply gets a ribbon for 'Participation'. Can you believe it? Talk about a nanny state.

June

18 Thursday

T20 first semi-final at Trent Bridge. Pakistan defeated South Africa. Apparently. The rest is a blur.

June

19 Friday

London

Shit. Punter's still not happy and both Vinny and Brute were giving me the evil eye all morning. The only thing I've been able to say in my defence is that I was looking after the new arrivals and so the late night of drinking was *technically* part of my leadership group responsibilities. Even so, I'm going to really have to keep a low profile for the next few days. Speaking of new arrivals, I had a good chat on the bus with Phillip Hughes this morning. Some are calling him the next Haydos!* But, as said to Boofa,** you've got to take this cricket caper one step at a time. It's important to cement your place in the team with consistent results and a trophy girlfriend before you go chasing big-name sponsors and publishing deals.

More corporate functions tonight, including a reunion dinner for those of us involved in the 2001 Test at Old Trafford. These are a regular feature on the cricketing calendar and I must say that organisers certainly do their research. Not only did they invite all of the players, umpires and ground staff involved in this classic encounter, they even managed to track down two blokes from Manchester who were fined for running onto the pitch during the Day 2 morning session.

Back at the hotel I checked my emails before going to bed only to be informed by my manager that the fall-out from last month's celebrity sports panel continues to be felt. This was an event I agreed to take part in before we left Australia, a league's club fundraiser in which a group of well-known sports identities get together and share humorous anecdotes. It was a decent line-up too: myself, Deano, Michael Klim and one of the tennis Woodies. Anyway, I made what I thought was a throwaway comment, an amusing quip about women's sport, not realising that two members of the Melbourne Vixens netball team were in the audience. Talk about a frosty reception, I was lucky to get out of there alive. Since then we've been trying to hose the incident down; I've written a letter of apology to both Netball Australia and the lesbian community but thanks to a few talkback radio hosts it's still causing fallout. The latest news from home is that Germaine Greer has weighed into the debate. Lesson learned. From now on I keep offensive comments confined to the dressing room.

* Wrong. The next Haydos was Pro (Phil Jaques).
** Provisional nickname – still waiting clearance from Darren Lehmann.

Rookies – Toddy's Take

When I started playing, senior blokes would give the new players a bit of a hard time as part of their initiation. It was an accepted part of the culture to test a rookie out by playing harmless practical jokes like dousing their kit in lighter fluid and setting it on fire, or not speaking to them for the first six weeks of an international tour. Of course, not all pranks were so lighthearted. On one tour of the Windies it was common practice to hide the new guys' helmets and other protective gear just before they went out to bat – and then watch on as they'd go out to face the inevitable 'chin music' with just one glove and a mouth guard (liberally smeared with wasabi paste, of course!). Great times. Nowadays if a debutante doesn't feel 100% 'comfortable', Cricket Australia start sending in 'transitional integration experts' to assist with their arrival. If you ask me there's nothing wrong with the older guys giving the younger pups hell, really making them earn their stripes. Letting them know they've got a long way to go before ever becoming a valuable member of the playing group. It builds team spirit and provides some much needed entertainment on a long tour. Provided these good-natured hi-jinks don't go too far (I personally draw the line at sexual degradation or loaded firearms), then they can only be good for the game.

June

20 Saturday

London

Training today was even more intense. In addition to our own guys we had plenty of net bowlers so everyone got a good hit-out. I've been watching Katto closely and I like the way he gets his head in position over the ball. This is something I feel will help me in the early part of an innings and I worked on matching his footwork. On a long tour such as this I think you can always pick up things from your team-mates. Often it's just tinea or a nasty cold, but today I came away with something more valuable.

Next I worked with Youngie, warming my arm up and throwing at targets. My power and accuracy have improved enormously since he joined the squad and I think in match situations this new-found strength will prove to be a real strength. Vinny then hit a few high outfield catches for us, one of which ended up in the car park – straight through the window of a brand new Daimler! Naturally we did the right thing and left a note, telling the unlucky owner to contact the England and Wales Cricket Board.

There's no doubt that having the entire squad together at last has made a real difference, along with the realisation that there's only another week or two before the first Ashes contest. For us this is the pinnacle: Test Match Cricket. It's everything those three words suggest. It's a *test* of a player's skills and focus. It's a *match*, pitting two sides against each other. And it's *cricket*.

The Australian team of 1948 were known as The Invincibles. After winning 10 Tests in a row a few years back we became The Dominators. Some cricket lovers have speculated what would happen if The Invincibles ever took on The Dominators. Of course, such a contest would be impossible because a lot of them are dead or really old, but if you adjusted for these factors I still think we'd tear the bastards apart. In a respectful way, of course.

I met the guys in the bar shortly after 7.00 pm before heading out for a meal at a nearby pub. I had the 600-gram fillet steak, which took a bit of getting through. By the time my plate was clean I had begun to regret ordering main course.

Back in the room I took out my diary and, based on everything we've learned so far, put together the Todd Ten Ashes Tour Commandments.

The Todd Ten Ashes Tour Commandments

1. Enjoy your cricket
2. Always give 100%
3. Acknowledge your mistakes
4. And those of others
5. Believe in yourself
6. Be competitive: hard but fair (mainly hard)
7. Play straight early in your innings
8. Come to team meetings in a positive frame of mind
9. And wearing pants
10. The only ball to worry about is the next one (unless you've just been bowled, in which case it's the last one).

290 Gloucester Road London UK SW7 4QH • T: +44 (0) 20 7373 1953 • F: +44 (0) 20 7370 5741

June

21 Sunday

London

I pulled up a little sore this morning, with swelling in my left knee. This knee has always been my Achilles heel, ever since I injured it during a Cricket Australia anger management seminar. Hopefully it won't get any worse, but I'll take today nice and easy just to be sure.

I tell you what, it's amazing what the press pick up on over here. The other day at training Sarfraz left the nets early with our physio to have some work done on his back. Twenty-four hours later and there's an article in one of the local papers with the headline 'Aussie bowler fitness scare'. Talk about jumping to conclusions! It's like that time a few years back in Sydney when some photographer got a shot of me being escorted from a nightclub wearing handcuffs and loaded into the back of a divvy van. Every journo in the country immediately assumed I was at the centre of some sort of 'incident'. Unbelievable!

Injuries – Toddy's Take

Injuries are part and parcel of a long tour. And they can happen anytime: on the field, at training, even on days off. Back on the '93 tour of South Africa, Tugga did his back riding a water slide in Sun City. Meanwhile during the 2007 World Cup Freddie Flintoff almost drowned after taking a pedalo out to sea at night. What does this tell you (apart from the dangers of rum)? Be careful. In my opinion you must limit physical activity to the absolute essentials of playing, training, golf and the occasional bat signing session. Anything more and you're just asking for trouble.

Tonight's T20 final involved two nations both touched by terrorism and civil unrest. In the end Pakistan were too good for the Sri Lankans and took home the cup. While I would naturally prefer it was us, it's good to see the Pakis with something to celebrate. The rest of the cricket world has shunned the place and I'm not sure whether any of us will ever visit there again. I have heard talk of a 2011 tour, subject to the ICC allowing us to bat with an armed runner, but even then I'm not sure too many guys would be keen to go.

While my batting exploits are well recognised, I feel I've been unfairly overlooked as a bowler of reasonable quality spin. For this tour I've even come up with a new ball, a zooting slider. It's basically my standard leg break, but delivered with an extra loud grunt.

June

22 Monday

London

With everyone's attention now fully focused on the First Test, a big open media session was organised for 9.00 am today, this time involving all of our Ashes squad. The boys are good at handling themselves in front of the press these days, thanks to the media training sessions organised by Cricket Australia at the start of each season. This, combined with the fact we are not allowed to personally answer any question without running our response by team management, means we generally stay out of trouble. If actually forced to speak I generally find the key is to avoid making specific comments about other players or officials. And, if you do, be sure to use the word 'allegedly' wherever possible.

After the media session we met with the match referee, Jeff Crowe, to go through rules and regulations for the upcoming series. This is something that happens at every tournament, a chance for us senior players to sit down and discuss any issues. The playing conditions are, in fact, circulated beforehand so the meeting is a good opportunity to ask the referee for clarification on any issue. Punter wanted the penalties for slow over rates explained along with rules for substitute fieldsmen. I wanted Crowe to explain why he fined me for dissent back in 2005 when all I did was linger at the crease for maybe 30 seconds tops because of an outrageous lbw decision that he really should have overturned.

One significant change for this series is that we will be abandoning the video referral system trialled during the recent South African series. This system allowed players to appeal by making a T-sign with their arms (as opposed to the traditional gesture of running towards the umpire, dropping to both knees, holding out your hands and screaming 'howizeeeeeee?' until red in the face). But the concept proved to be more trouble than it was worth. For a start, the technology simply wasn't up to scratch; during the First Test Duminy was clearly out, caught behind off Sidds. Big appeal from our keeper – that should have been enough. Big appeal from the bowler – confirmed it. But no, 'not out' says Bucknor. So BJ does the reasonable thing and lodges an appeal. Turns out the video umpire has a 'problem with camera five'. It wasn't even on, meaning that the batsman got the benefit of the doubt and we were robbed of a wicket. Leaving aside such technical hiccups, I don't like the system because of its delayed nature. Waiting endlessly for an off-field umpire's decision can wreck the momentum of a fielding team's celebrations. By the time a batsman is given out you've already finished congratulating each other and can easily forget to give him a decent send-off. Not good for the game.

We had the rest of the day off so a few of us decided to head out. I feel it's important when on tour to escape the four walls of your hotel room and, wherever possible, immerse yourself in the culture and history of a new country. We spent the afternoon in a nearby sports bar watching Kent play Hampshire in the county Twenty20 Cup, before heading on to a steakhouse for dinner.

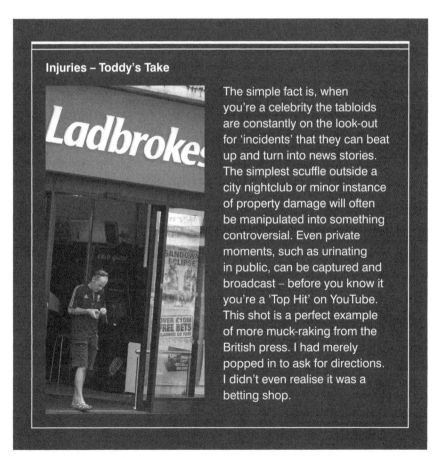

Injuries – Toddy's Take

The simple fact is, when you're a celebrity the tabloids are constantly on the look-out for 'incidents' that they can beat up and turn into news stories. The simplest scuffle outside a city nightclub or minor instance of property damage will often be manipulated into something controversial. Even private moments, such as urinating in public, can be captured and broadcast – before you know it you're a 'Top Hit' on YouTube. This shot is a perfect example of more muck-raking from the British press. I had merely popped in to ask for directions. I didn't even realise it was a betting shop.

June

23 Tuesday

Hove

An early start this morning because the team was due to check out and head south to Hove, a seaside town on the coast of England where we are scheduled to play our first tour match against Sussex. I overslept a little and ended up being about 20 seconds late for the team bus. This is going to cost me, as the social committee of BJ, Katto and Mitch love to fine us for any minor breach of team rules (I'm still paying off a series of missed team meetings from 2004).

To make it easier on our selectors, the Poms have agreed to relax the rules on team numbers, meaning we can field 12 players tomorrow. They have, however, refused to relax the rules on umpire abuse, so we'll have to be on our best behaviour. It's no secret that Sussex is very much a third-string attack, but we'll still need to be careful. It's easy to become complacent when you know you're facing a B-grade team, such as a President's XI or New Zealand, and let your guard down. So we'll be treating them with a fair bit of respect (at least for the first few sessions). While there's a bit of competition between our batsmen, tomorrow's match is really being billed as a show-down for our bowlers. Age is the big factor with Bing. At 33 he's still as fast and fired up as ever, but there are little signs that time might be catching up with him. This morning in the rooms he complained that he could 'feel a draught'. In terms of injuries, we have a few concerns regarding Watto. A recurrent knee problem has ruled him out of tomorrow's practice match, news the big fella has taken in his stride. However, the announcement that he may also miss this weekend's golf day has not gone down so well. Also sitting this match out are Ronnie and Choco.

Another net session this afternoon. These are generally optional the day before a match but, with the selectors yet to finalise our batting line-up, I wanted to impress and so I told Mitch, Sidds, Hilfy and Bing to really charge in at me. I didn't mean it of course, I was just trying to show off in front of Punter, but the bastards all let fly. A few bruised fingers later and I was actually looking forward to the gym.

An interesting issue was raised at tonight's team meeting – our choice of headwear for tomorrow's game. Ever since the outcry in Jamaica last year when we fielded in VB caps, this has become a vexed issue for tour games. A lot of the boys who are yet to make their Ashes

Test debut would prefer not to wear the baggy green. But some of the other blokes don't like fielding in floppy hats either. After a lengthy discussion (including a PowerPoint presentation on the subject from Vinny) it was decided to settle the matter via a telephone conference call with Cricket Australia back home. Unfortunately this didn't leave us a lot of time to talk tactics for tomorrow, but I think the general team philosophy was summed up by Punter who handed us some thoughts he had jotted down about the upcoming series. His words were simple: 'We will approach each match 100% focused. Our aim is to play at our best, all the time, every time. We will work towards being the best skilled team the world has seen – technically, physically, mentally and tactically. Our mission starts now …' Pretty stirring words, and in no way diminished by the fact they were written on the back of a beer coaster. Let the play begin!

Injuries can strike at any time on tour – this was sustained during a team meeting. From now on only the captain and members of our leadership group will be allowed to use the laser pointer.

June

Sussex v Australia (Tour match)
Hove
Day 1

The ground was bathed in sunshine when we arrived this morning, meaning we should get four days play. Mind you, this is England so it could just as easily be snowing by the first drinks break. Punter won the toss and we elected to bat so as a result our bowlers' 'shoot-out' would have to wait for a day or two. Boofa got things underway with a blaze of boundaries, racing to 15 before having his middle stump removed. A flurry of wickets then followed – Punter (8), Snorks (1) and Huss (32) – as we slumped to be 5/114 shortly after lunch, before Katto and I managed to steady the ship.

I've got to say, it felt good to be out in the middle again. I guess I just enjoy the game so much, the competition, the one-on-one battles. When I'm batting I relish the idea of it being one against 11. Or one against 12 if you take into account the mood Katto was in after I almost ran him out in the first over. I pushed a ball into the covers and I really thought there were two in it, especially as the bloke fielding was carrying more than a few extra kilos. But that's the thing about fatties, they can often move surprisingly quick, whether on the field or in a lunch queue. I made it to 50 in pretty good time, bringing up my half-century with a full-blooded six over long on. There's no denying it, belting balls out of the ground is a magical sensation, even though there's always that faint concern you might clock someone in the crowd. I've hit a few people over the years: a sightscreen attendant, a couple of school kids and a lady in Perth who was reading a book (and therefore deserved it). We ended the day on 7/349, a pretty decent score. What's more, most of us batsmen got some pretty valuable time out in the middle, with the obvious exceptions of Punter, Boofa and Snorks who were, frankly, disappointing.

Back at the hotel the news on Watto was not good; according to the latest scans he has a definite tear in the thigh muscle and management have admitted we may need to call up a replacement (batsman, not thigh), who will most likely be Brad Hodge. This is devastating news for our talented all-rounder, especially as he was only just coming good from that groin strain and his left knee was definitely on the improve. Leaving aside his suspect right shoulder, chronic lower back condition and suspected heart murmur, the big fella has never looked better.

Running between wickets requires sharp reflexes, stamina and, above all, excellent communication skills. When passing at high speed you've got less than a second to tell your partner 'one more!', 'keep left!', 'I've got a stitch' or 'sorry, my mistake'.

My motto, whether having made a duck or run over someone's cat, has always been 'never look back'.

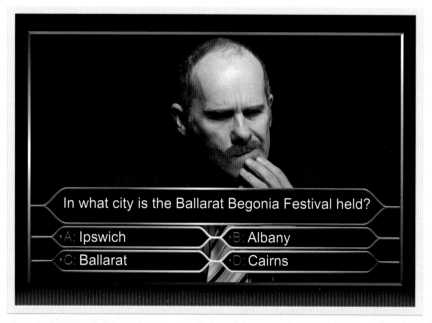

My appearance on the celebrity version of Who Wants to Be a Millionaire *was unfortunately cut short after I was stumped by a particularly tough question in round one.*

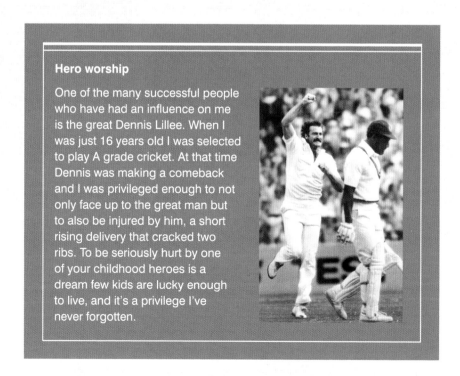

Hero worship

One of the many successful people who have had an influence on me is the great Dennis Lillee. When I was just 16 years old I was selected to play A grade cricket. At that time Dennis was making a comeback and I was privileged enough to not only face up to the great man but to also be injured by him, a short rising delivery that cracked two ribs. To be seriously hurt by one of your childhood heroes is a dream few kids are lucky enough to live, and it's a privilege I've never forgotten.

The ToddBall™

Before using the ToddBall™ make sure:

1. You maintain good posture
2. There are no cuts or damage to the ball
3. There are no cuts or damage to you
4. Drink plenty of water
5. Refrain from alcohol (unless experienced)

Warning:

www.WarwickTodd.net takes no responsibility for any damage/injury caused by following the exercises described within this site or if you roll off and hit your head or the ball bursts or whatever, so don't even think about suing because you'll lose. It is recommended that you consult with your doctor or physio before using the ToddBall but don't be put off by any alarmist warnings.

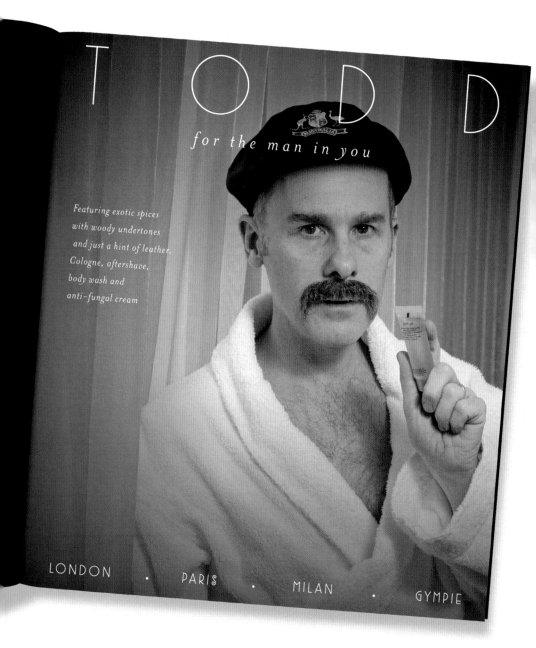

TODD

for the man in you

Featuring exotic spices
with woody undertones
and just a hint of leather.
Cologne, aftershave,
body wash and
anti-fungal cream

LONDON · PARIS · MILAN · GYMPIE

Regrettably, my signature aftershave had to be pulled off the shelves after some do-gooder consumer advocacy group found a possible link between its active ingredient methylene chloride and damage to the central nervous system of rats. It's not meant for rats! Anyway, the good news is it's still available for sale in the Northern Territory.

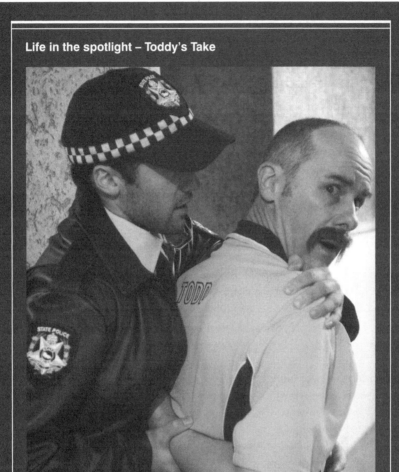

Life in the spotlight – Toddy's Take

I don't think people who are not in the public spotlight can even begin to realise what it's like dealing with media scrutiny, day in day out. The knowledge that, every time you step out of a restaurant or bar, there will be paparazzi waiting to take your photo for tomorrow's newspaper. And the added burden of having to notify them in advance to make sure this happens. It takes its toll. Spare a thought for those of us who face the realisation that everything we do will be watched, whether it is walking down the street, going to a movie, or simply being loaded into the back of a divvy van.

June

25 Thursday

Sussex v Australia (Tour match)
Hove
Day 2

We declared on our overnight score, meaning it was time for our bowlers to really stretch out and show what they could do. Which, as it turned out, proved to be bugger all. Hilfy claimed an early wicket but didn't achieve much from then on. Bing soon had 8 against his name, but unfortunately these were no-balls, not wickets. Sidds was workmanlike and Sarfraz generated some decent pace, flooring their wicket-keeper at one point with a magnificent throat ball. But despite our best efforts, Sussex made it to 311, including 22 runs from no-balls. Bing was easily the worst offender, followed by Sidds and Hilfy, but even Haurie managed to overstep the line three times. Vinny was seriously pissed off, warning our bowlers that no-balls could be the deciding factor when it comes to selection for the First Test. It's not easy when you're in the field watching your team-mates get carted round the ground. Naturally you can keep up a steady stream of 'well bowled' but after a while it can stop sounding completely genuine.

The other worrying feature of our bowling today was the fact that half of their score came from fours and sixes, meaning we were clearly bowling too many loose balls. When I say 'we' I don't include myself as, despite a lot of warming-up movements and other obvious visual hints, Punter refused to offer me the chance to unleash a little Todd off-spin. Of course, it's his decision, but I think it's the wrong one. Not only can I be very accurate, I have an unorthodox, zig-zag follow-through which means all you've got to do is let me change ends and I can bowl into my own footmarks. Instead, Punter stuck with Haurie who ended up going for 98 runs, including 16 in one over just before lunch. Our front-line spinner was understandably disappointed but Vinny and Punter assured him he was still very much in the running for the First Test. I think he bought it.

Disappointing news back at the hotel when I was approached by our media manager who said a few journalists had asked him about an allegation that I had sworn at some children on my way onto the ground this morning. I do remember the entrance to the playing arena being lined with kids holding flags, and I might have said something lighthearted as I was passing through, but to suggest that I called one of them a 'fat dead-s—t' is absolutely false. If I did use such a phrase, it almost certainly would have been directed at one of their parents. Anyway, he promised to deal with it and we all headed out to a local restaurant for a few drinks and dinner.

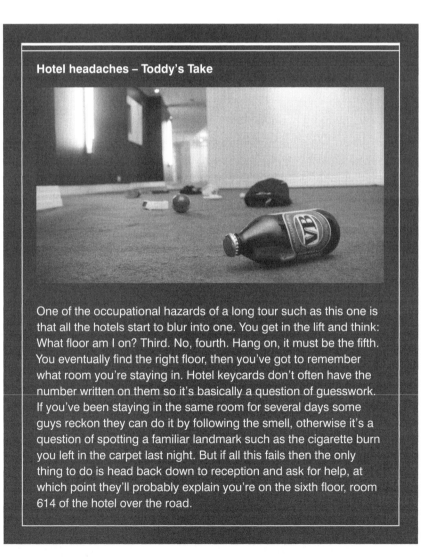

Hotel headaches – Toddy's Take

One of the occupational hazards of a long tour such as this one is that all the hotels start to blur into one. You get in the lift and think: What floor am I on? Third. No, fourth. Hang on, it must be the fifth. You eventually find the right floor, then you've got to remember what room you're staying in. Hotel keycards don't often have the number written on them so it's basically a question of guesswork. If you've been staying in the same room for several days some guys reckon they can do it by following the smell, otherwise it's a question of spotting a familiar landmark such as the cigarette burn you left in the carpet last night. But if all this fails then the only thing to do is head back down to reception and ask for help, at which point they'll probably explain you're on the sixth floor, room 614 of the hotel over the road.

Sussex v Australia (Tour match)
Hove
Day 3

We resumed this morning on 0/18 and watched as Punter, Boofa and Pup all made brisk half-centuries. In fact, most of us got a start and enjoyed some valuable time in the middle, with the exception of Snorks at number six who managed only a scratchy 11 to go with his 1 from the first innings. The West Australian left-hander took 22 balls to get off the mark and rarely managed to strike the ball with the middle of the bat, eventually being adjudged lbw to the final delivery before tea. Watching on from the rooms we could tell the big fella was not happy with the decision and we acted quickly to remove all breakable items from within reach, but I'm afraid to say the Sussex Cricket Club may need to look at replacing some crockery, along with a couple of door hinges and a photo of the Queen (or Club President – it was hard to tell).

The other downside of today was yet another failure from Huss. Not that you'd call 40 a 'failure' (and in hindsight I regret using the term during my post-match interview), but he took nearly three and a half hours to scratch out these runs. Hardly a polished innings by his standards, but still a step in the right direction. I was relegated down the order to give some of the other guys a chance at the crease, and we ended the day on 7/379, setting Sussex 418 for a win tomorrow.

Because of the time difference between England and Australia I am forced to deal with a lot of issues back home overnight. This evening I was on the phone to my lawyers for about an hour trying to sort out problems with a current business venture. My brother Damien and I have recently got involved in property developments, buying up old industrial or contaminated land sites and turning them into residential developments. Our first site, Lake Edge Estate, sold really well (thanks, no doubt, to the television ads I fronted) but now it seems that several buyers want out, claiming 'false advertising'. As I explained to the lawyer, at no stage did we claim there was an actual lake on the development site, but according to him they could have grounds for taking action. We're now looking at the possibility of pumping tertiary effluent into a low-lying section of the estate and renaming it Lake Style Estate, but there still could be issues. I really don't need this sort of distraction in the middle of an Ashes tour, but what can you do?

Cold comfort

After a long day in the field we're supposed to all take ice baths as part of our post-match process. For those not familiar with this form of torture, it basically involves lowering yourself into a wheelie bin full of ice. The theory is that it helps with muscle recovery but in my opinion it's just another one of these sports medicine fads, like stretching or alcohol-free days, that I hope will one day be abolished. In the meantime, we play, we freeze.

June

27 Saturday

Sussex v Australia (Tour match)
Hove
Day 4

After another long day in the field we agreed to draw stumps three overs early, with Sussex on 7/373, just 45 runs short of their target. It was a good day for Ritzy, who bounced back from the hammering he took in the first innings to take a wicket. He should have had two after Hopkinson spooned a dolly to mid-wicket but Punter dropped an absolute sitter. Had it been anyone else, the bowler would have cursed, glared and then spat but, seeing it was his captain at fault, the most Haurie could do was grin and laugh it off. The other big performer today was Sidds who really bent his back, finding extra bounce in the wicket and all but booking his place in the First Test team. Unfortunately, Bing had another no-ball shocker. It started in his first over with the new ball when he was belted for two fours before getting an edge from Chris Nash – only to have the umpire indicate no-ball. Of course, the big paceman was halfway down the pitch by this stage in the middle of a full-throated victory dance and, as a consequence, didn't get the no-ball message for about three minutes, at which point he seriously looked like overstepping the mark again, this time in the direction of umpire Malone.

Whether he's taking wickets or not, Bing is one member of the team you can always count on to give 100%. (He was once said to have given 112% but this may have been wind-assisted.)

In all, Bing's opening spell produced three no-balls for no wickets and Vinny was clearly not happy during our post-match meeting. By way of defence Bing argued he had been 'let down' by poor fielding, a comment made while looking rather obviously in my direction. But, as I've always said, fielding is about conserving energy. You get a lot of showy young players, darting after every ball, desperate to cut off singles or turn fours into threes. It might produce a grateful nod from the bowler but by the end of the day these eager outfielders will hardly be able to move. I'll run if it's really necessary, but not in the final session of a soon-to-be-drawn tour match. And besides, bowlers have to realise that the only reason the ball has been hit into the outfield is because of their substandard performance – so let them chase it.

Despite not actually winning we were still pretty pleased with the outcome and spent a few hours after stumps listening to music, having a few quiet drinks and generally enjoying the feeling of our first victory since the T20 practice match against New Zealand. Then it was onto the bus for the trip to Worcester.

Even in tour matches, the order in which a side walks off the ground is carefully regulated, with first place reserved for the best performing player. There was controversy today when Sarfraz (0 for 50) pushed ahead of Snorks (2 for 80), causing a huge row to erupt in the rooms. I missed the actually controversy as I was busy checking messages from sponsors.

June

28 Sunday

Worcester

We arrived here in Worcester last night, the venue for our next tour match. Following a sleep-in and a short recovery session in the gym, the morning was spent relaxing at the hotel. After the luxury of London, this place is a little less suited to our needs and a few of the boys have reported problems with their rooms. Watto's hairdryer isn't working and apparently Pup doesn't have enough mirrors. Our team manager, Brute, was called in to fix things and immediately dealt with the situation by finding someone else to deal with it.

I went out to grab some lunch at a local café with Bing, Mitch and a few of the new boys. I keep getting reminded that a lot of these blokes have never toured before. When the bill arrived Choco actually got up to pay it! We had to explain to him that a quick photo with the manager and a couple of signed serviettes is generally all that's required, but it was a close call.

After a quick team meeting we were given the afternoon off and a few of the boys decided to catch some movies. We saw *State of Play* (not bad), *Night at the Museum* (crap) and *Watchmen* (didn't really understand it, so probably crap).

Disappointing news today that several other members of the squad are also working on tour diaries. I won't name the individuals responsible, as it could be embarrassing when their various book deals fall through, but I will have to be a little careful with sharing anecdotes and insights, just in case they get 'borrowed' by someone else looking to fill a chapter or two. At least I can say that this diary will be written by Yours Truly. You wouldn't believe the number of players who use so-called ghost writers to help get their thoughts down on paper. I even tried it myself once, a few years back, when we were thinking of putting out an autobiography. My manager got this bloke in, some ex-journalist by the name of Lawrie Colvin. The two of us would meet once a week and I'd talk about previous tours, all the things I'd got up to, amusing stories and my various run-ins with the authorities. The idea was that he would then go away and put it all together into a decent book. Instead, he went away and published an unauthorised biography; a tell-all exposé that I then had to spend the next six months telling people was all crap – not easy when most of the information had come from me. (In the end we organised for an *authorised* unauthorised biography to sort of set the record straight, but by then the horse had bolted.)

There are some laundry items that are definitely 'hand-wash only'.

June

29 Monday

Worcester

The team for our next tour match was named today, with no real surprises. Sidds has been rested, a pretty sure sign that the selectors see him as a definite starter for the First Test. Hilfy is also out, meaning he's got no chance. Ronnie was really hoping for a spot but he's been overlooked again, meaning there's no way he'll play in the First Test. It was hard to tell how the big Victorian took the news; he locked himself in his room and refused to let anyone in. Punter eventually managed to convince him to open the door by posing as a room service attendant wanting to re-stock the mini-bar.

The facilities here in Worcester are pretty good and we spent the morning in a lengthy net session. Despite solid performances at the crease against Sussex I still like to work on the basics of footwork and timing. For me, batting is largely about instinct. You rely on muscle memory and fitness, not thinking. In fact, the less inclined you are towards intellectual activity, the better you are at it, which probably explains why players like Pup and BJ have been so successful over the years.

One familiar face at training today was Aussie Formula One driver Mark Webber who was invited to drop in by Punter. Being part of the Aussie squad you get used to seeing famous figures hanging round the hotel and rooms. Pop stars, politicians and Olympians are all common visitors. While it's good to meet and mix with other high-profile figures, there are times when the constant stream of celebrity well-wishers can get a little distracting, especially when they keep coming back. During some recent Sydney Test matches we had to boost security at the dressing room door just in case Russell Crowe showed up again.

At the team meeting tonight we discussed the spate of no-balls that plagued us during the recent tour match against Sussex. Our coach, Vinny, made it quite clear that this was not in any way intended to be a 'witch-hunt' or attack on our fast bowlers, although it was telling that none of them were actually invited to the meeting. But there's no denying their bowling display did bring back bitter memories of our 111 no-balls during the 2005 series – including 39 in the Fourth Test loss at Trent Bridge. We also discussed our opposition, the England Lions (formerly known as 'England A') who are basically the country's second XI. Our former coach, John Buchanan, is currently employed as their adviser so they'll probably be holed up in a conference room tomorrow reading quotes from Chinese philosophers, meaning we can hopefully have the practice facilities to ourselves.

The A list – Toddy's Take

The exposure to famous people is one thing you soon get used to as a member of the Australian cricket team. But there are still times when I have to pinch myself! For a country kid who left school at 15, to be sitting in the same room as a semi-finalist from *Australian Idol* or having the team from *Coxy's Big Break* want to visit your beach house for their 'Celebrities-by-the-Sea' segment (which, I might add, was then dropped from the actual show despite us doing all the weeding) can be a little overwhelming. Over the years I've chatted with everyone from prime ministers to pop stars, not to mention my fair share of high-profile female fans. This shot was taken before last year's Allan Border Medal presentation that I attended with weekend weathergirl Ebony Pritchard. Halfway along the red carpet and we'd already been dubbed Australian cricket's new 'glamour couple'. Unfortunately, things went downhill from there; I got drunk and she ended up heading home with a Young Cricketer of the Year nominee.

June

30 Tuesday

Worcester

We woke today to discover that the English press were up to their old tricks again, printing stories about 'in-fighting' and 'feuds' within the Aussie camp. Honestly, where these so-called journalists get their facts from beats me. One alleged source was quoted as witnessing a 'heated argument' between two players outside a popular restaurant. Total crap. Look, there are some pretty strong personalities in any squad and to suggest that we all get on all of the time would be false. That said, there's a real sense of camaraderie amongst anyone who shares the baggy green, and reports of feuds and fights are generally exaggerated. Rarely are voices raised or punches thrown (unless it's after dark) and, when two players do clash, they are encouraged to resolve their differences quickly and in the appropriate fashion, by getting their managers to sort things out.

An optional training session this morning saw most of the guys turn out, eager to fine-tune their skills ahead of tomorrow's game. Even though it's only a tour match I'm determined to be at my best. As a cricketer I've always endeavoured to give 100%, whether at the crease, in the nets or merely attending a sponsor's product launch.

Before each training session and practice game on this tour, an Australian cricketer has been invited to stand before his team-mates and share his recollections of Ashes series past. Some have read from prepared scripts, some have free-styled. This morning it was my turn and I chose to address the guys in the form of a poem.

B is for the Batsmen who lead our team with pride,
A is for the Awesome way we sweep and cut and glide.
G is for the Guts we show when we go out to play,
G is for the Guts we show when we go out to play.
Y is for the Yorkers that our bowlers sometimes bowl,
G is for the Guts we show when we go out to play.
R is for the Runs that flow when we stay at the crease,
E is for the Effort that will never ever cease.
E is for the Effort that will never ever cease,
N is for the Nowledge that we always play to win,
Put them all together and you've got the BAGGY GRIN.

Now I'm no wordsmith but I think these words had a pretty profound effect on the boys and, by the time I'd finished, the rooms were in complete silence. Admittedly a few of the team had left to start their stretches, but you could tell that those who stayed for the whole poem were pretty moved.

We were joined at training by about 30 under-19 local guys keen to spend a bit of time with us. After a solid net session a few of the guys not so badly concussed were invited into the rooms for lunch and a chat.

While that was happening Punter gave a press conference. One of the announcements was that Watto would not be playing due to his injured thigh. The big all-rounder didn't even train with us today, and was confined to walking laps of the ground with our physio. It's a tough break for Watto who has had a terrible run with injuries, having missed games through groin strain, stress fractures in his back, a dislocated shoulder, hamstring strain and knee damage. Some critics have labelled him 'weak' and point to the fact he once sat out an entire World Cup campaign due to a bad haircut. But I know Watto and with just a little bit of luck, along with enough cortisone, he'll be back in no time.

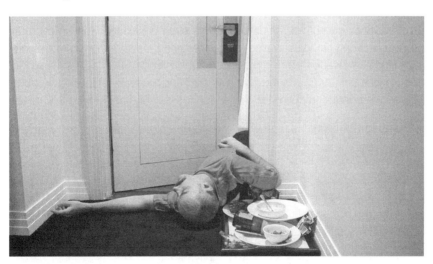

Sometimes on tour you just need to order room service and spend a quiet night in.

July

1 Wednesday

England Lions v Australia (Tour match)
New Road, Worcester
Day 1

Perhaps the most unusual feature of today was the weather; unlike the cloud and drizzle we are normally used to in England, it was warm and humid when we arrived at the ground. In fact, one newspaper described it as being 'more like Wagga Wagga than Worcester'. It was so hot that by the time play started the ground announcer declared that gentlemen might officially loosen their cravats. We won the toss and decided to bat. Things got off to a fiery start with Steve Harmison striking Boofa on the head with his very first ball. Our young opener was then out a few deliveries later to a classic throat ball for just 7. Punter went for only 1, a worrying off cut played on the back foot with a straight bat; he's been out in this manner before. Pup made it to 4 and Snorks a disappointing 1, and so when Huss arrived at the crease he was under a fair bit of pressure. A lot of nasty things have been said about Mr Cricket's lack of form in recent months (although, in my defence, I've only ever said them when he's not around) but today he answered those critics with a fine century. Katto also played well, getting out on 95 just a short while after lunch to a combination of good bowling and the effects of the second pastie he decided to have. I went cheaply, caught behind trying to sweep. Losing your wicket in such circumstances, there's no point blaming the pitch (which was grossly substandard), or the umpiring (I've seen better decisions in D grade cricket) or even your team-mates (I was only trying to move the run rate along after Huss and Katto had hogged most of the innings). The fault rests almost entirely with you, although the light was bad and we really should have been offered the chance to come off. We ended the day on 8/337, not a bad result.

After play – Toddy's Take

My post-match recovery routine is fairly standard. An ice bath, a quick rub down on the physio's table, a couple of beers and then I'm ready to relax or face whatever disciplinary hearing I've been summoned before.

Back at the hotel a few of the boys were keen to grab a bite but I chose to have a quiet night in. To be honest, I've always found it hard to go out and enjoy myself on days when I haven't performed well on the field. Obviously if there's a major team function or free drinks somewhere then I'll push myself, but generally I prefer to lie low. In the past, whenever I went through a rough trot on tour, I'd phone my wife Ros. She used to offer advice, not so much technical as psychological, because she read a lot of self-help books and would tell me that a big innings was mine for the taking if I simply harnessed my inner sense of positive yes-energy, stayed in the moment and stopped myself from truth-gating. And avoided playing across the line.

While very enthusiastic, the England Lions were clearly inexperienced. Despite my low score not one of their players remembered to give me a decent send-off. (One of them even said 'bad luck' – can you believe that?)

July

2 Thursday

England Lions v Australia (Tour match)
New Road, Worcester
Day 2

We were quickly dismissed this morning for 358, at which point Worcester's openers, Stephen Moore and Joe Denly, set about compiling an opening stand of 175 runs. Punter tried everything, but Bing, Mitch, Sarfraz and Haurie all got hit around. I made a few suggestions to our skipper, mainly relating to fielding positions and which end our bowlers should be operating from. In reply Punter made one suggestion to me, mainly relating to shutting the f@*k up, and I spent most of the next session fielding on the boundary. About half an hour before tea, Punter spotted Bing down on the fence chatting with a few members of the crowd. Our captain was not exactly happy with this and gave his (wicketless) paceman a real serve, or 'bollocking' as the Poms would call it. Well, it seemed to do the trick and Bing responded with a blistering spell of anger and aggression. Mainly directed at Punter to begin with, but he then managed to channel this fury into his bowling. In fact, his first ball hit Moore absolutely plumb, although the umpire somehow thought there was bat in it. But this didn't stop Bing who soon had Denly (66) and then Bell the very next ball for a duck. With the big fella on a hat-trick, we naturally brought the field up but somehow new batsman Vikram Solanki just managed to hold the ball out. Each of Bing's victims was sent on their way in vintage style, with a few well-chosen words of advice and an angry stare, although he reserved his biggest glare for Snorks who chipped in late for the sixth wicket, depriving Bing of sole wicket-taker status. The day ended with the home team at 6/302.

The exciting news is the way we managed to produce consistent reverse swing, a weapon the Poms used with such devastating effect on us back in 2005. This is something that would no doubt have been spotted by selector Andrew Hilditch, had he actually been watching, and not been on his phone for most of the afternoon session.

After a long day in the field a few of the boys were understandably keen to head out for a drink but, being a little older, I'm now more interested in getting to know the unique history and culture of each city we're staying in. Tonight I visited Worcester's oldest pub.

Each day before play a different member of the squad is invited to read a short passage or quote out that the boys can think about on the field. This morning Katto read from 'The Prophet' by Kahlil Gibran, something about 'trees not growing in shade'. Two overs later BJ was back in the sheds, so confused he played over the top of a slower delivery. It's now been agreed we'll stick to reading simpler material, such as each others' tour diaries.

Being successful in the field is about doing the one percenters, those little things that lift a team. It's assisting the bowlers, whether with a word or two of encouragement, or by running across the pitch and leaving marks for them to land the ball in.

Gatorade is not only our official energy drink, it's also our official supplier of reverse swing.

Which batsman walks off the ground first at the end of a session can be a tricky issue. Here, Punter had made 17 more runs than me, but my strike rate was well above his so I went first. He didn't speak to me for the rest of the match.

A well-chosen comment, word or even sound effect just as the bowler reaches his delivery stride can be devastatingly effective.

It's not unusual for a player to have a word or two with the umpire as he's walking off the field. In this case it was three words, two of which cost me a significant fine for offensive language.

Friday

England Lions v Australia (Tour match)
New Road, Worcester
Day 3

While the papers were full of praise for Bing and his five-wicket haul yesterday, I took exception to a report in the *Guardian* that said: 'the Australians worked hard on the ball yesterday, in ideal roughing conditions.' I'm not sure exactly what they meant, but if the implication is that we in any way tampered with the ball, or altered it in an illegal way, then this is something I can categorically deny. It is perfectly within the rules of cricket to polish one side of the ball, and many players do this with a dry cloth or bit of rag. I personally find a small sheet of sandpaper equally effective, but all we are doing is maintaining the ball in optimum playing condition.

Rules of Cricket – Toddy's Take

3. The match ball – changing its condition

(a) Any fielder may
(i) polish the ball provided that no artificial substance is used and that such polishing wastes no time;
(ii) remove mud from the ball under the supervision of the umpire;
(iii) dry a wet ball on a towel.

As this rule clearly states, no *artificial* substances may be used to polish a ball. However, the polish I prefer to use is made out of beeswax, a 100% natural ingredient. Still, try telling the umpires this.

England resumed this morning on 6/302 and we managed to knock them over without too much trouble for 352, with Sarfraz, Mitch and Bing all sharing in the wickets. Our second innings got off to a shaky start when Boof went for 8, bounced out for a second time by Harmison, then Punter followed a few balls later for just 15. Shortly before lunch I found myself out in the middle, eager for one final hit-out before the First Test. As expected, I was greeted by a few short-pitched deliveries, with Harmison in particular keen to give me a working over. On 37 I was surprised by one that bounced a little more than expected; I tried to pull out of the shot but made that decision too late, and the ball ended up squashing the grille of my helmet onto the right side of my face. There was no pain, but pretty quickly I began to feel something trickling down the side of my face, and when I looked at my shirt I could see blood dripping onto it. Our physio was quickly on the scene with his usual assortment of bandages, gaffer tape, pain-killers and power of attorney forms, but I was able to bat on for the remainder of the session, ending up with a confidence-boosting 53.

The highlight of our afternoon session, apart from my determined knock, was Snorks reaching a century. It's been a fairly dry run spell for our number six and he was so excited at achieving triple figures that he leapt in the air, kissed his helmet and looked towards our dressing room to share the moment with his mates. I felt bad that none of us had been watching (we had a game of 500 going at the time) but we've all promised to check out the highlights package on TV tonight.

We ended the day on 4/276, giving us a tidy lead of 282. A surprise visitor back at the team hotel was Pigeon who was in the London doing some promotional work when he realised he still had some credit left on a drink card from Worcester in 2005 and so decided to head up and claim it. It was good to catch up with a fellow veteran of the team and re-live a few memories, although when he started trying to sell us all signed copies of his autobiography we had to pretend there was a team meeting scheduled. Back at the hotel team management had decorated our meeting room with dozens of emails, faxes, postcards and letters of encouragement from fans back home. Many were addressed to me personally and all were positive, apart from one or two overdue electricity bills that must have somehow snuck through. Hopefully we don't let the cricket lovers of Australia down.

July

4 Saturday

England Lions v Australia (Tour match)
New Road, Worcester
Day 4

The headline in one paper this morning read 'Hughes and Ponting Fail', which, if you ask me, seemed a bit over the top. Tour matches are supposed to be an opportunity for us batsmen to play ourselves in with some quality time at the crease and I'm sure both Boofa and Punter benefited greatly from their few minutes there.

We batted on for a session, allowing Snorks to reach 191 not out and Pup 80. The only scare was when Huss was struck on the ankle and forced to retire hurt, but he seemed to have no trouble getting to the head of the luncheon buffet queue so I don't think the injury is too bad. The England Lions then struggled to reach 4/162, with wickets being shared between Mitch (2), Bing (1) and Haurie who finally managed another scalp. I don't know who was more surprised, the batsman or bowler, but we certainly made a point of celebrating Haurie's achievement, just in case it was the last time he gives us the opportunity. The game ended in rather unusual circumstances when umpire Jeff Evans fainted shortly after turning down a strong appeal for leg-before. It was certainly a full-blooded shout but I've never seen someone actually collapse before.

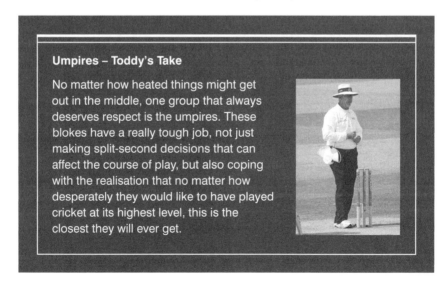

Umpires – Toddy's Take

No matter how heated things might get out in the middle, one group that always deserves respect is the umpires. These blokes have a really tough job, not just making split-second decisions that can affect the course of play, but also coping with the realisation that no matter how desperately they would like to have played cricket at its highest level, this is the closest they will ever get.

After four days in the field it was time to catch up on some emails and other paper work before heading out to dinner. More frustrating news from my manager back home regarding my future (or lack of) with the Channel 9 commentary team. Ever since the great Richie Benaud announced his retirement earlier this year we've been in talks with Channel 9 about W. Todd stepping into a senior on-air position. We even went to the effort of recording a professional audition tape that was express-posted to them months ago. But apparently the reply has just come back from some 'Assistant Producer' (aka shit-kicker) along the lines of 'thank you, but we already have a tape of Mr Todd'. As I pointed out to Neville, that tape was taken outside a Chapel Street nightclub and I don't think it fully showcases my broadcasting talents. Neville has promised to keep trying and, if anyone can make something happen, it's my manager.

Just managing

One of the most important decisions an international player can make today is his choice of manager. You need someone with a thorough understanding of negotiation tactics, contract law, employee rights and martial arts, who has a wide network of contacts and can be relied upon to consider the best interests of his client at all times. Such people are rare, which is why I was so lucky to find Neville Gulliver. His shrewd business instincts, honed by 22 years in the boat trailer business, coupled with an honesty that has seen him walk away from three separate ATO investigations without a conviction, make him the perfect man to represent my interests.

July

5 Sunday

Cardiff

Okay, I'm a bit hazy-headed this morning. We ended up having a big night out to celebrate the end of our second tour match, along with the fact that we've finally got to leave Worcester. Myself and a few of the boys kicked on a little late, breaching team rules that say we players have to be back at the hotel by midnight. I argued (unsuccessfully) that I was back at a hotel, just not our team hotel, but this was ignored and I copped another fine. We're now in Cardiff, the venue for the First Test in just a few days. The people here are Welsh, quite friendly and many of them speak English, but pretty fast so you've got to pay attention.

Cardiff is, of course, famous as the city where our former team-mate, Roy, first jeopardised his international career by turning up for a match against Bangladesh showing the effects of a long night's drinking. I remember Punter, Buck and Brute spending an hour and a half during the solemn bus ride to Bristol discussing a suitable punishment for Symmo, and the following day it was announced he would be fined $4000 and banned for two games. (He was, however, allowed to continue his role as head of the social committee.) Since then, we've all been very careful about overindulging.

Heavy rain this morning forced us to hold a net session indoors. While the facilities here are good, it's never quite the same batting inside; the pitch surfaces are different and you can't spit so it can be hard to truly replicate match conditions. After getting back from the ground I grabbed a bit of lunch at a place across the road from the hotel. As always on tour, I'm careful with what I eat. We've got enough problems to contend with just staying injury free; the last thing anyone needs is food poisoning. Luckily it's not such a problem here as it is in Third World destinations such as Pakistan or New Zealand. Although the worst place would have to be India. During the '07 tour, three-quarters of the team went down with gastro. One Aussie player was so badly affected that his bathroom was officially declared a crime scene.

This afternoon brought the moment every member of the Australian squad dreads. Bat signing. For those not familiar with this ritual, Cricket Australia basically put about 500 bats in a large room at the hotel and lock the doors. We are then forced to sign each and every one of them. Most are for sponsors, some go to charity, I believe one was even part of a hostage ransom bid; some British aid worker being held by the Taliban in Pakistan who would only be freed in return for an autographed willow. But whoever the bats are for, it's an absolute pain to sign them all and I have known players over the years who will do anything to get out of the ordeal, even if it means paying someone else to do it for them. It's rumoured that 99% of bats bearing Mark Waugh's signature were actually signed by a junior member of our coaching staff. Over the years I've discovered that the trick is to come up with a quick signature. Maybe just the first letter of your name and then a squiggle. Fortunately 'Todd' is not so bad. Imagine if you were Vangipurappu Venkata Sai Laxman or Inzamam-ul-Haq? The Sri Lankan team apparently have to set aside a month for bat signings and, despite extensive training and warm-ups, routinely lose players during the process through repetitive strain injuries.

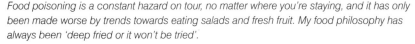

Food poisoning is a constant hazard on tour, no matter where you're staying, and it has only been made worse by trends towards eating salads and fresh fruit. My food philosophy has always been 'deep fried or it won't be tried'.

July

6 Monday

Cardiff

Our planned training session at Sophia Gardens this morning had to be cut short due to the weather. Heavy rain pretty much limited our options to indoor net work and games of 500, both of which really brought out a competitive streak in the boys. Having been dismissed twice in tour matches by bouncers, Boofa has been doing quite a bit of extra work against the short ball. Understandably, a lot of guys have been offering advice but, if you ask me, this can be dangerous. I've seen too many blokes tinker with their action and get themselves in all sorts of trouble. Cricket's a simple game. You make runs. You take wickets. You celebrate with a few cold drinks at the end of the day. Then face the match committee hearing. Anything else is just a distraction. Boof just has to put his early indifferent form behind him and remember what got him into the squad in the first place. Talent. And the fact he's from New South Wales.

Punter spoke to us this morning in the dressing rooms about what it takes to win. The words that came out of his mouth were amazing. It made the hairs on my neck stand up and the nerves and anticipation just rose to the next level. You can really tell whenever he speaks, he speaks from the heart and he really knows what it takes. On that note, throughout the tour, we've all had the opportunity to tell the group what it means to play in the Ashes. Huss came up with a poem about the Ashes, which was really clever, especially the way he managed to rhyme Cricket Australia with genitalia.

The next player to talk was Pup, although he didn't actually say a word. Instead he put together a presentation on the big screen (with some help from resident video guru Mick Marshall no doubt) about what it meant for him to play in the Ashes. He had heaps of photos ranging from the Ashes urn to a shot of England holding it in '05. Then us holding it in '07. Then some shots of his fiancée Lara holding it that really got the boys fired up. It was quite an amazing little presentation and not a word was said while he was going through the slideshow. In fact, we sat in complete silence (broken only by the sound of a couple of our fast bowlers snoring). Things like that really do nail down how important this series is for us.

Finally, Punter got up (again) and took some time to recall events that had stuck in his mind. Moments like Junior's (Mark Waugh) hundred over here, Tugga's (Steve Waugh) hundreds in both innings, Merv (Hughes) bowling bumper after bumper amongst other things. I felt he might have mentioned my 167 on a green seamer at Edgbaston but obviously that match-saving performance has been conveniently overlooked, which is perfectly understandable; when you put in such extraordinary performances so consistently I guess it's easy to take them for granted.

This afternoon we received the shock news that Bing had been ruled out of the Test match line-up with a side strain. He pulled up with a sore left rib after the tour game at Worcester and went to London today for scans where the diagnosis was not good. According to the medicos it seems he might have tried too hard, or 'over-exerted', in an effort to impress the selectors and ended up straining an internal oblique muscle. It's a real danger in lead-up games, which is why I always make a point of pacing myself (or 'under-exerting'), keeping something in the tank for the main event. Anyway, Bing is understandably devastated, especially as he feels like he's let the side down. Which, of course, he has, but there's nothing we can do about it now. At least he made it back to Cardiff in time to be in the official Ashes Squad photo, although I must say this one seemed to take forever. First the photographer wasn't happy with light, then Pup's stylist wasn't happy with his hair. Finally we got the thing shot and were able to head back for the team dinner. These are traditionally held two nights before the match starts, and are a chance for the boys to relax as a group before the 'battle' begins. To lighten the mood we were entertained by a magician who was absolutely brilliant. One trick he performed just blew everyone away. He took team manager Steve Bernard's credit card and somehow managed to get it hovering and spinning in mid-air. There were no wires anyone could see and none of us could figure out how he did it, not even the blokes drinking light beer. The show was great value and the perfect way to end our night. Why, then, a few of us decided to go clubbing is a little hard to explain but it was a good opportunity to relieve a few pre-Test tensions.

First Test Team Meeting: Player Notes

* Congrats to Haurie and Hilfy, well done guys
* Bad luck Sarfraz (no one to tell him we had this meeting)
* This is it – cricket's biggest challenge
* Let's show commitment, desire, pride, will to win, fire in the belly
* Remember the three Ps – Patience, Pressure, Partnerships
* And Performance. That's four.
* No-balls still a problem; need to eliminate
* No quiet times – intensity, activity, energy
* Be ruthless – make them feel unwanted
* Test goes for five days – hang tough, be the man
* Match theme – let's go one up, no excuses, we want nothing short of a win
* Or at least a draw
* Partnerships are the key! Don't lose two quick wickets
* Attack key bowlers (Flintoff, Anderson)
* Respect all bowlers (Broad, Panesar)
* Don't worry about Swann.

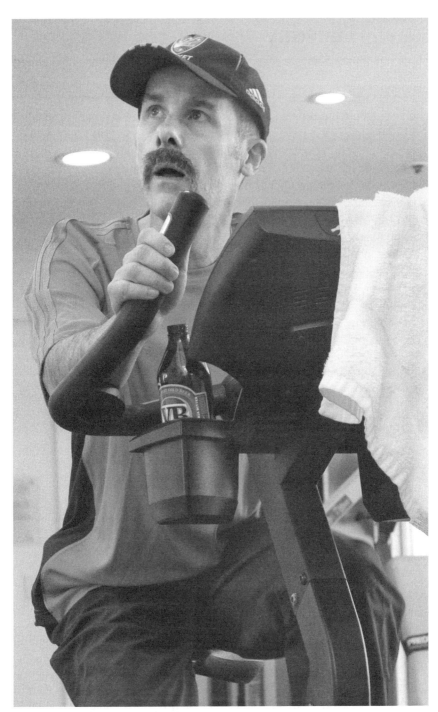

When working out in the hotel gym I always make sure to keep my fluids up.

July

7 Tuesday

Up early today for our final training session before the big game. With the selectors yet to decide on the team, everyone was keen to impress; I noticed a few of the boys had even shaved. Of course, this could also have something to do with the fact that a few more partners and wives have arrived in time for the First Test. One of the other effects of the girls being round is how the atmosphere on the team bus suddenly changes. There's less horseplay and fewer dirty jokes. On the way to the ground this morning I even saw Sidds actually reading (or pretending to; the magazine was upside down). But whatever the case, I know from experience that on a long and gruelling tour, players can benefit enormously from the love and support of a beautiful wife. Preferably their own. One piece of bad news – Steve Bernard's credit card has apparently been stolen and someone has used it overnight to rack up close to £5000 worth of purchases.

Following a solid workout at Sophia Gardens we made a close inspection of the pitch. After the past few days of rain this is about the only dry patch of ground in Cardiff. Punter is still unsure whether to enter the Test with an all-pace attack or select spinner Nathan Hauritz. Of course, that's a decision for him and the selectors, and I won't be interfering, other than leaving the odd anonymous Post-It note on his hotel room door to help clarify a few options.

We had a team meeting at 10.30 am to make sure we were all clear on our plans for tomorrow. As usual, we went through the opposition line-up in detail with a few relevant thoughts, along these lines:

- Andrew Strauss – loves to play square of the wicket on both sides, so make sure we bowl full and straight to him. Do not be afraid to let him have a short ball.
- Kevin Pietersen – very strong on the on-side so try to maintain a disciplined line on or outside off-stump. Do not be afraid to let him have a short ball.
- Andrew Flintoff – loves to hit fours and sixes so try to keep him quiet with defensive fields. Do not be afraid to let him have a short ball.
- Ravi Bopara – can't bat to save himself. Do not be afraid to let him have a short ball.

In terms of a batting plan, the aim is to make as many runs as we can early, then some more in the middle of the innings, followed by quite a few towards the end. As far as batting plans go, I don't think this one has changed that much since 1989.

Punter ended the meeting by asking everyone to make sure they are switched on for the next five days – not that we need much encouragement on that front! One thing I'll be making sure to do is set the old alarm clock. One of the greatest fears for any touring player is sleeping in and missing the team bus. This has happened to new players like Bryce McGain as well as experienced campaigners such as Slats and Roy. I came close in the West Indies once when, after a big night on the rum punch, I completely forgot to set the alarm. The only thing that saved me was the fact that I had (luckily) fallen asleep underneath the team bus, meaning I was there for the roll-call, albeit hung-over and in thongs.

The Standard

PUBLISHED IN MELBOURNE SINCE 1854   WEDNESDAY, MARCH 25, 2009 $1.50 INC GST

Cricketer in Car Tram Collision

Charges Pending

Yet another media beat-up, with this outrageous article claiming that I crashed my car into a Melbourne tram while answering a phone call. Let's get a few facts cleared up, shall we? 1. The tram crashed into me. 2. At the time of the alleged impact the phone was hands-free (I was holding it between my knees). And 3. I did not 'run' from the scene of the accident, I was simply late for an appointment and decided to leave my car there on its roof until the morning. Of course, none of this made it into the article, with the journo responsible following the time-honoured rule: never let the facts get in the way of a good story.

July

8 Wednesday

England v Australia (First Test)
Cardiff
Day 1

On the day of a match I like to get up around 7.30 or 8.00, which made the 4.35 am wake-up call something of a shock. Vowing to get back at the boys responsible I rolled over and managed a few more hours' sleep before it really was time to get up.

Heading in on the bus I made a point of having a chat with Boof. For all his obvious natural ability and outward confidence our young opener is about to face one of the biggest challenges of his career – an Ashes Test match – so I thought it might be worth just trying to help him prepare mentally for the event. I told him about a few of my own experiences and how I thought he might best approach the day. I must say, he seemed remarkably calm and very relaxed. Turned out he was asleep.

As always there were quite a few fans at the ground waiting for autographs when we arrived. I usually say 'no' on match days as it's important to stay focused but I always make an exception for people with disabilities, such as those in wheelchairs or the seriously fat. One kid spoke to me and I couldn't understand a word he was saying so I assumed he had some sort of major speech impediment. Turned out he was simply speaking Welsh.

Contrary to some reports, I do not charge for autographs, apart from a small administrative fee to cover costs.

England won the toss and elected to bat, with Mitch taking the new ball. Our frontline paceman immediately settled into his recent rhythm, the first delivery wide, slow and failing to swing. It was Hilfy who made the breakthrough, getting Cook for 10 to a corker of a catch from Huss. A few more wickets saw the Poms heading to lunch three down. During the next session Punter decided to give Haurie a bowl but, as feared, he didn't really trouble the batsmen and proved quite expensive during his long spell from the River Taff end. It's times like this that body language can be very important for a fielding team. If the man at the crease looks round and sees you with shoulders drooped or arms crossed, moving slowly to position between overs, then he can easily get a psychological edge. That's why, no matter how badly our bowlers are performing, I work hard to keep the intensity up. Lots of talk, encouraging words, brisk movements – these are all the things I tell our 12th man he should do while I'm off the field having a rub-down and waiting for some sort of breakthrough.

After lunch, Haurie picked up his first wicket. He was understandably over the moon about capturing this scalp and, even though some commentators felt the lap of honour may have been taking things a little too far, we were pretty pumped up for him too. With none of their players able to go on to build a big innings, the Poms ended day one on 7/336. Not a bad result for us and, provided we can grab some early wickets tomorrow, I think we're pretty well placed.

Today saw the induction of Tom Graveney, Peter May and Ian Chappell into the ICC's Cricket Hall of Fame. The crowd at Cardiff stood to applaud these three legends of the game and, watching on from the pavilion during lunch, I couldn't help wondering would I one day be joining this exclusive club. Not that you play the game for awards or accolades, but it's nice to be acknowledged. Just last year I was nominated at the Laureus Sports Awards for 'Comeback of the Year', narrowly losing out to some French skier who returned to his sport after losing both legs in an horrific accident. No hard feelings, he was a worthy winner (although I think he might have played a little heavily on the sympathy vote, and he was given artificial legs – I'm still out there batting with the same groin).

All in all a great start to the 2009 Ashes series, and a day played in the true spirit of Test cricket.

July

9 Thursday

England v Australia (First Test)
Cardiff
Day 2

Arriving at the ground this morning I was shocked and disappointed to be told that a charge of racial abuse had been levelled at me by umpire Aleem Dar who claims he heard me making 'offensive comments' yesterday to English batsman Ravi Bopara. I honestly don't know what he's talking about. Yes, I was fielding in close and may have said a few things relating to Bopara's batting technique (or lack of!) but anyone who knows me knows that I would never say anything racist or offensive about a person's ethnicity, and it's just so typical of a Paki umpire to get it wrong. Naturally I'll be denying the charge.

ICC Code of Conduct – On-Field Abuse Charges

Level 2.6 = offensive abuse not amounting to racism
Level 2.7 = racist abuse not amounting to an offence
Level 2.8 = racist abuse amounting to an offence
Level 2.9 = what Darren Lehmann called the Sri Lankan team
on 15 January 2003

Our plans to dismiss England quickly and cheaply this morning did not exactly eventuate, as their tail pretty much ran amok, allowing them to reach a massive total of 435. Things were looking good when Mitch claimed Broad in the fourth over, but then Swann and Anderson mounted a vicious counter-offensive, blasting 68 runs off only 53 balls for the ninth wicket. Swann was particularly tough on Haurie, smashing him for three consecutive boundaries in his first over, which ended up costing us 16 runs. Haurie began his spell with men around the bat but the field gradually dispersed. By lunch there were two of us in close, eight on the boundary and one waiting in the car park to help retrieve the next six.

After finally taking the last wicket it was our turn to bat, with our openers Katto and Boof given the tough job of negotiating the eight overs before lunch. As expected, Boof was subjected to a string of short-pitched deliveries and did well to reach 36 before Flintoff managed to get an edge. The successful bowler then celebrated this wicket by running with arms outstretched, soaking in the adulation from fans who were by this stage at fever pitch, baying for blood. It was like a soccer crowd back in Australia, only no one had set fire to a Macedonian flag or let off a flare. Fortunately, Punter and Katto were then able to steady the ship and, by the end of the day, they had both gone on to post magnificent centuries. Katto had a life on 56 when he should by rights have been given out lbw, but a ton is a ton and there's no taking that away from him (even if it was absolutely plumb). We naturally gave them both a standing ovation when they returned to the rooms having guided us to 1/249.

No matter how well someone's played there's no reason they shouldn't be given a decent send-off.

10 Friday

England v Australia (First Test)
Cardiff
Day 3

To hear your name, 'Warwick Todd', announced over a ground's loudspeaker system is a truly spine-tingling moment. Hearing it followed by the phrase 'please report to the match referee' slightly takes the gloss off the occasion. But it still capped off what could only be described as a great day for us.

We arrived at the ground full of confidence, with Punter and Katto well set and ready to go on with things. Huss was padded up and looking keen to get out in the middle himself. I must say, for a man seriously battling form, Mr Cricket seemed surprisingly up-beat and confident in the rooms. I went over and had a chat, asking him about his string of recent failures in South Africa and general inability to build a decent sort of Test innings, in particular the fact that he has only made one half-century in his past 13 Tests. By the end of our conversation I sensed he was looking a lot more focused.

We lost three wickets against the new ball; first Punter, who chopped a cut shot onto his stumps shortly after reaching his 150. Then paceman James Anderson claimed Katto for 122, followed by Huss who was caught behind driving for just 3.

Shortly after lunch I found myself walking to the crease to join Pup who was on 23. It felt great to be out in the middle once again, and I had little trouble keeping the old scoreboard ticking over. No doubt the England bowlers were beginning to tire a little, and the ball was not doing all that much off the pitch. Perhaps it was the ease of scoring that led to me dropping my guard a little and, on 37, spooning the easiest of catches to mid-on. Predictably enough I was given a fearful send-off. Normally such a thing wouldn't bother me but this one came from my own batting partner. I guess Pup was hoping the two of us could build a really impressive stand. As it turned out, rain interrupted shortly after and the afternoon session was actually resumed under floodlights (a first for a Test match in the UK)*. We moved on to be 5/479 at stumps, a lead of 44 runs.

*Interesting fact. To check light levels the umpires employ an interesting technique – laying the ball on the ground. If they can see that the ball is casting a shadow then it is considered too dark to play. If they can't see the ball at all then it's definitely time to come off.

Pup and I were involved in another near run-out today when he shouted 'yes!' and I thought he was calling for a quick single; turned out he was merely excited at seeing himself on the big screen.

Sometimes in the heat of battle simple misunderstandings can escalate. Flintoff thought I'd just made an offensive remark to him. I was, in fact, speaking to the umpire.

July

11 Saturday

England v Australia (First Test)
Cardiff
Day 4

We go into this fourth day in a pretty strong position. Obviously there has been a lot of focus on the centuries made by Punter and Katto (at last night's team debrief we were all made to watch the Sky News highlights package twice), but I think the most pleasing aspect of our performance yesterday was how well all our middle order did, especially when you consider that the last time many of us held a bat for any sort of extended period was the team signing session.

On our arrival at the ground this morning the greatest obstacle to victory seemed to be the weather; the forecast was predicting heavy, driving rain easing to a light deluge by evening. With this in mind we declared on 6/674, a lead of 239, hoping there would be enough uninterrupted periods of play for us to dismiss the Poms.

As it turned out there was just enough time to snare two quick wickets. Alastair Cook was trapped plumb in front on 6 by Mitch and then Ravi Bopara was also adjudged lbw to Hilfy on 1. To be honest, the ball may have been missing leg stump and the batsman was a long way forward, so it was a fairly muted appeal; only about nine of us went up and just three players actually got down on one knee. But the umpire declared it out, meaning they were two down and trailing by 219 runs when rain terminated play at tea. And we have 98 overs tomorrow to dismiss them.

Back at the hotel, senior team management received a bombshell with the news that Mike Hussey has formally requested a new nickname. After an extended period of low scores he feels worried that 'Mr Cricket' could start to sound sarcastic. We've told him not to make any rash decisions while the matter is referred to a committee for further discussion; in the meantime he'll be referred to as 'Mr Hussey'.

Fielding – Toddy's Take

Some batsmen find it boring when they're not actually at the crease but I take my role in the field very seriously. The aim, when fielding, is to increase pressure on the batsman by forcing him to face dot ball after dot ball. You then try to join those dots together into a maiden and, if possible, extend this string of maidens into a session, a session into a day. Eventually the batsman will get so frustrated that he'll either play a rash shot or take up a more exciting sport.

July

12 Sunday

England v Australia (First Test)
Cardiff
Day 5

As feared, I woke this morning to the sounds of a torrential deluge but fortunately it turned out to merely be the hotel fire sprinkler system that one of the boys had somehow managed to set off in the corridor outside my room. There had, in fact, been heavy rain overnight, but by the time we reached the ground the skies were clear.

During our warm-up, Mitch had to be physically restrained by Pup when England's Kevin Pietersen hit a ball into his path. Pietersen claimed it was an 'accident' but Mitch reckons he could tell it was deliberate. Those of us on the last Ashes tour are still suspicious about that ball Pigeon twisted his ankle on during the warm-up, another so-called 'accident' that was never fully explained despite our repeated calls for a Royal Commission.

Hilfy managed to bowl Pietersen in the fourth over, then Haurie got Strauss for 17 but England's Paul Collingwood somehow managed to occupy the crease for almost six hours. Mitch was pretty loose, I wouldn't say he 'wasted' the new ball, but he did, and Haurie was also ineffective. Punter tried everything: switching bowlers, changing ends, moving the field around. He even gave me a turn with the ball and I had two good shouts, one for leg-before off my third delivery and another when Punter decided to replace me with Snorks. As the final session wore on things started to get fairly tense out in the middle. I was cautioned by the umpires after making shoulder contact with Stuart Broad mid-pitch, although it was really quite innocent. You often get a fielder running into

Luck – Toddy's Take

In my mind too many poor players blame a lack of success on luck. Good players know to blame the umpires, the pitch or inadequate practice facilities.

the path of a batsman and, as long as both players clearly have their eye on the ball, there's no problem. Admittedly this collision took place during a drinks break but there was honestly nothing in it.

We eventually got rid of Collingwood but England managed to hang on, reaching 9/252, thanks to the pair of James Anderson and Monty Panesar along with some fairly dubious time-wasting tactics. Now I'm not going to say that England breached the spirit of the game but they clearly did. In the tense final overs of the match they twice sent on 12th man Bilal Shafayat and their physio with spare gloves for Anderson who had (allegedly) spilt drink on them. If this wasn't an obvious stalling tactic, the appearance of their 12th man a few balls later with deodorant and a toothbrush was clearly going too far.

Naturally I accept the fact that batsmen are entitled to slow the pace of an innings down a little. But you do this in the accepted fashion, with frequent mid-pitch conferences and extensive gardening. You don't summon support staff out onto the field. Punter, obviously furious, let his feelings be known but to no avail, and England held on for a somewhat questionable draw. Towards the end the crowd was cheering on every dot ball and maiden over, with both batsmen receiving a standing ovation as they walked off at the end of play.

Punter was awarded Man of the Match, a decision greeted with boos from the crowd – rather unsportsmanlike if you ask me. (Call me old-fashioned, but I was brought up to believe that spectators should always respect the opposition – you only boo umpires, ground attendants and police.)

There were mixed emotions about today's result. Clearly we have been the better side for the past five days, and we will take many things away from Cardiff, including a heightened sense of self-confidence as a team, along with a set of bronze ceremonial goblets I managed to pinch from the visitor's dining room. We are also in a good position injury-wise, with none of us showing niggles or other problems, apart from BJ's tinea which has apparently flared again (he blames the rain). But there is a nagging sense of failure that we were simply not good enough to completely finish the Poms off. Of course, it would be easy to blame our bowlers for this, so that's what we agreed to do, before heading out for some post-match celebrations.

July

13 Monday

London

The war of words over yesterday's time-wasting episode has escalated overnight, with England coach Andy Flower accusing the Australian captain of deliberately inflaming the incident. Flower went on to rather pointedly mention that England had twice won the International Cricket Council's 'Spirit of Cricket' award in the past four years, something Australia 'was yet to do'. As anyone who follows this award would know, Australia has been nominated on several occasions, only missing out on winning due to the vagaries of the voting system (and the fact that I've generally been in the side).

Of course, this is all really just part of the psychological gamesmanship that goes with a tensely fought Ashes campaign and you can be sure that when the time comes Punter will respond the best way he knows how (via his column in *The Daily Telegraph*). We headed back to London last night and are all looking forward to a few days off before the Second Test. Quite a few more of the wives and girlfriends have joined the group and it's good to see them soaking in the culture and history of London, mainly by purchasing shoes. There's no doubt having the girls around can be a positive influence. Back in the days when we toured without partners things could get, let's just say, a little wild. Hotel room parties and one-night stands were commonplace for a lot of the guys. This said, let me state for the record that, on all my trips away with the Australian squad, I was never unfaithful to Ros once. Twice, yes, and there was a certain tour to the West Indies when I bagged a hat-trick, but those decadent days are now a thing of the past.

Tonight on London's Southbank we attended a major fundraising dinner in aid of the Ponting Foundation. As a senior member of the squad I was asked to say a few words. Not being great at this sort of caper, I have spent most of last week working on a few ideas, including a couple of good anecdotes and some amusing moments from the tour so far. In the end I had the makings of a pretty entertaining 15 minutes. However, Punter insisted I run the speech past our media officer who, in turn, insisted I drop a few sections. I was then left with barely a minute. If you ask me, this is yet another example of political correctness gone mad. When a person can't get up and make a few lighthearted remarks about the Royal Family, comments that are clearly intended as a joke (no one is really going to think Her Majesty would get a corgi to do that sort of thing), you have to ask yourself what the world is coming to.

The official purpose of the function was to launch a fundraising campaign called 'Run Ricky Run' in which every run Punter scores in the Ashes Tests will trigger a donation to one of his foundation's beneficiaries. It's a well-intentioned idea but, in my opinion, things can go wrong. I launched a similar scheme during the summer of 2004–05, pledging to donate a percentage of player payments to a well-deserving cause. Unfortunately, by the time we deducted match fines Kidney Australia were $23,000 in debt and trying to back out of the scheme. Stick to raffles I say.

Cracking the Code

Everyone in the Australian team knows how important the spirit of cricket is to the way we play the game. So, in 2003, we players agreed it was time to get serious, and wrote our own Code of Conduct. I was part of the initial drafting committee and, let me tell you, it was one of the most extensive and strictest set of rules since the Geneva Convention. Under our recommendations a minor misdemeanour would attract an immediate warning. A more serious or repeat offence could see a player fined up to 1.5% of his match fee plus the threat of the possibility of the potential for a fine. For truly grave on-field offences (i.e. anything involving legal charges or a coroner) we suggested a verbal rebuke. At this stage Cricket Australia stuck their nose in, insisting that a few of our penalties may have been a little on the lenient side, so they were ramped up again, making the Code an even stronger blueprint for lasting change. We drafted the Code in November 2003 and agreed that it would come into effect the following month – giving ourselves one last Test (in Brisbane) to really cut loose.

The Players Code of Conduct, along with its subsequent amendments The Players Code of Conduct (Sledging), The Players Code of Conduct (Spitting), and The Players Code of Conduct (Andrew Symonds), form a cornerstone of how we play the game. It's our guiding manifesto, what the Bible is to Christians, the Koran to Muslims or the *Karma Sutra* to Hindus.

July

14 Tuesday

London

It was a slow start this morning as quite a few of the boys were still recovering from yesterday's recovery session. As usual, training was scheduled and where better than at Lords, the home of cricket. Even after all these years I still get a thrill arriving at this historic ground, with its magnificent gates and stands each bearing the name of great cricketers from years gone by. Compton, Edrich, Grace, Investec. I'm not sure there'll ever be a stand named after Warwick Todd (although the possibility of a bar at the MCG has, apparently, been raised) but we can always dream.

I must say, the facilities here at Lords take a bit of getting used to, and one local paper reported that Victoria's 'boy from the bush' Peter Siddle got completely lost making his way from the dressing room to the nets. Mind you, I've seen Sidds get lost at breakfast just making his way back from the toaster, so it's hardly front-page news.

Apart from training, today was all about settling into what will be our new home for the next week. For those of us who have played here before there's a sense of familiarity about the Lords dressing room. The worn benches, the wooden lockers, that sweet-smelling scent of linament, sweat and cigarette smoke that seems to follow the Australian team. We cricketers are creatures of habit and a lot of the guys who have played here before immediately took up their old positions. Katto and Punter along the back wall, Pup and myself facing the balcony, Bing out back on the physio's bench.

Looming above us all was the famous honours board listing every overseas player who has scored a century or taken five-wicket hauls in an innings here. Seeing the name W. Todd carved up there during the 2005 Ashes Test still ranks as one of the highpoints of my professional career, even if it was removed the following day by ground officials who subsequently charged me with wilful damage and confiscated the penknife.

We had a really good team meeting tonight, focusing on the many areas in which we were deficient in Cardiff, such as all the wides we conceded, the lack of spark with the new ball, slow over rates. In the end it's possible we may have focused a little heavily on the bowler's faults, which could perhaps explain why they stormed out early, but Punter was able to lure them back with the offer of some free chips. Vinny then spoke about his impressions of the First Test, saying that he felt we were missing a couple of key ingredients: enjoyment and hunger. (At this stage I could have mentioned that I was also missing my room key, but I didn't feel its loss had directly impacted on team performance.)

As usual before a Test we went through the England squad, with our coach presenting a detailed profile on each player. In the old days there simply weren't the resources to study opponents in depth; we thought it was pretty good if anyone could remember whether a bloke batted left- or right-handed. Now we've got statistics, strength analyses, wagon wheels and even video footage, all designed to help us target any potential weaknesses. So, for example, tonight we were reminded that Andrew Strauss loves to play square of the wicket, tends to hook in the air, and could be gluten-intolerant. He's also a Sagittarius.

Second Test Team Meeting: Player Notes

* Time to step up a gear, be the man!
* Let's make sure we have respect for England
* No, seriously
* Maintain standards: discipline, passion, aggression, hustle
* Batsmen; let's put pressure on their bowlers
* Bowlers; line and length, first 10 overs crucial
* Fielders; hunt in packs, no quiet times, take and make half-chances
* 12th man; wash Gatorade bottles properly
* 7.50 departure tomorrow morning
* Theft of concierge's top hat, culprit to return, no questions asked

July

15 Wednesday

London

As always, the day before the start of a Test match is kept deliberately low-key so that players may prepare in whatever way they like. Back in 2005, a team picnic was organised in Hyde Park as a way for everyone to relax and 'switch off' for a few hours. Unfortunately that lunch was followed by a social hit of cricket that turned a little ugly after one player's girlfriend copped a short-pitched delivery and several of the boys ended up almost trading blows. Speaking of partners, the English press are still questioning the wisdom of Cricket Australia allowing the girls to be part of the Ashes tour, claiming their presence could prove a distraction to us players. The latest newspaper article has been prompted by revelations that a new group has just been formed, the Australian Cricketers' Wives Association, and that certain key members could be demanding a say in team selection.

This afternoon most of the boys chose to hang out at the team hotel. I used the opportunity to catch up on emails, something that can very quickly spiral out of control if not sorted out on a regular basis. There were the usual bunch of charity requests, including yet another one from the Blind Cricket Association of Australia who want me to be guest speaker at their annual dinner later this year. I originally said 'yes', mainly to get them off my back, but now that the date is getting closer I've decided I'm simply too tired to drag on the monkey suit and front up at some reception centre for another feed of overcooked beef. So last week I made them an offer; I'd record a speech and they can just play the tape. It's not like any of their guests are gonna know I'm not actually there. But they're still insisting I show up. I may have to handball this one to Neville.

The only 'formal' event today was an optional session with the team psychologist who got us to practise a technique called 'positive visualisation'. Basically it involves us all sitting still and thinking about the game ahead. You have to see yourself walking out to the wicket, imagine that you're taking guard and then hitting the first ball to the boundary. This form of mental preparation is supposed to be highly effective but, I'm sorry to say, I fell asleep halfway through the session. Worse, I had a dream that we lost inside three days. Might stick to net practice.

Well, tomorrow it's on to Lords. According to the history books, we haven't lost a Test there since 1934. And I certainly don't intend to be part of the first team to break that record run. We've done all the training, all the hard work and preparation, now there's nothing more to do ...

If the cap fits

The baggy green. It's more than a piece of cloth. Just as the martial artist has his black belt, or the stripper her red crotchless undies, so too is this our badge of honour.

Not so many years ago there was no ceremony at the handover of a cap. In fact, a lot of players got theirs in the mail. But now it's a full-on affair, with everyone lining up before the start of the game and a past player invited in to say a few words. This makes the occasion quite special although you have to be careful about your choice of player as some old timers can go on a bit. I remember one baggy green presentation a few years back that involved a 30-minute rant about declining standards of player behaviour (the phrase 'in my day' got a serious work-out). In the end the toss had to be pushed back half an hour. This sort of ceremony is a far cry from the day I first got my cap. It was simply stuffed in a bag and left outside my hotel room door, along with a reminder to settle the mini-bar bill before check-out. But despite this lack of ceremony I still treasure it. Of course, after 15 years my baggy green cap looks pretty tattered and torn, and it smells horrible – a legacy of sweat, blood, spilt beer and that time I fell into a Sri Lankan sewerage canal. Luckily you don't notice it so much 'cos the rest of my cricket gear smells pretty much the same.

Interesting fact. Tugga wore the same cap for his entire career. Towards the end it had become so worn and damaged that he actually had it repaired by Albion, the original hat makers. They put new felt on the peak and re-glued some of the seams, before steam-cleaning and reinforcing the sides with stitches (interestingly, this was the exact same procedure Graham Gooch and Warnie had done on their scalps).

16 Thursday

England v Australia (Second Test)
Lords
Day 1

Except remember to set the alarm clock. I honestly don't know how I managed to sleep in on the morning of a Lords Test, but it happened. Luckily I was woken by shouting in the next room (Mitch was on the phone to his mum) and I just managed to make the bus by skipping a few 'luxuries' such as shaving, showering, breakfast and underwear.

There was a real buzz on the streets around Lords as crowds flocked into the ground. As usual, a huge contingent of Aussies were there, including fans, journos and quite a few ex-players either leading supporters tours or doing commentary work. Drawing the biggest crowd outside the ground was – you guessed it – Warnie, who is now calling the match for Sky TV. Watching our former champ being mobbed outside the gates I was reminded once again of how tough it is for Warnie – everyone wants a piece of him. Fortunately, when it comes to the female fans, this feeling tends to be mutual.

While Punter was completing his final media duties, the rest of us warmed up in the nets. I then gathered the boys into a circle where I made the announcement that Andrew McDonald was about to make his Lords Test debut. Ronnie's reaction to the news summed up how much this place means to Australian cricketers – he choked up at the thought of achieving something he'd dreamt about for years. So genuine was the big Victorian's emotion that we almost felt bad telling him a few minutes later it was a joke.

Looking across to where the England team was warming up we could see that fast-bowling spearhead Andrew Flintoff was hobbling about with a massive amount of strapping on his right knee. Not a positive sign for the Poms, especially as that knee was his good one. But not long after, the official teams were announced and 'Freddie' took his place in the line-up.

England once again won the toss, choosing to bat on what looked like a pretty good wicket. Hilfy was given the new ball, which he took as quite an honour until he realised that this meant he would be bowling uphill. His first delivery was slow, widish down leg-side and bounced twice before reaching BJ, pretty much summing up our day with the ball.

Things only got worse when Mitch took hold of the pill; his first 11 overs conceded 77 runs, including 15 boundaries. This slightly loose spell allowed openers Strauss and Cook to get off to a pretty good start, amassing an opening partnership of 196 runs. The papers described it as a 'historic stand' but, when you think about it, the Poms have been crap for so long that just about anything they achieve on the field can be called 'historic' as, chances are, they won't have done it for at least half a century. Sidds was also a bit wayward and we could do little but watch as Strauss cruised to another (historic) century.

On Day 1 at Lords I was fined for excessive appealing, a decision I intend to appeal.

16 Thursday

Punter tried speaking to our quicks between overs but this can be fraught with peril. It's one thing to wander over, pat a paceman on the arse and pretend to say 'well done champ' while you deliver instructions, but if you linger too long then the batting team will sense that things are not going well. Because of this you never want to get into heated conversation or start waving your arms about. And, above all else, keep it brief. Unfortunately, as the session wore on Punter found himself with more and more to say. Things peaked just before the luncheon adjournment when, during one mid-wicket conference, he called for chairs and someone to take minutes.

But the message must have eventually got through and several wickets fell in the afternoon session, including those of Bopara, Collingwood and Pietersen. I was directly involved in one of these dismissals, a sharp chance from Flintoff when he miscued a shot off Hilfy. I ended up taking the catch just a few centimetres off the ground and apparently, from some camera angles, it looked as if the ball may have actually hit the ground. Of course it hadn't. I was confident that the catch was fair and indicated this fact to the umpire in the standard fashion – by not waiting for his decision and immediately starting to high-five and hug my team-mates. Eventually his finger went up at which point the batsman lingered at the crease, which I thought was very unsportsmanlike, especially as by this stage I'd run all the way over to point out where his dressing room was.

During the afternoon session there was a security scare when a woman (far right) somehow managed to get onto the Lords members balcony.

There was a real scare for us during the afternoon session when Ritzy dropped a sharp return catch and then fell to the ground clutching his finger. When he got up it looked pretty bad, bent back at a hideous angle; from where I was standing he looked like umpire Billy Bowden. Ritzy appeared to be in all sorts of bother, signalling to the dressing room and almost vomiting with pain before going off. On the plus side, the ball began showing signs of reverse swing late in the day, surely a good sign for tomorrow.

England ended the day on 6/364, with their captain unbeaten on 161. As Strauss walked off there was a standing ovation from the crowd and, naturally, quite a few handshakes from the Australian team. Some commentators later complained that we Aussies were merely shaking each other's hands which, while true, is really just splitting hairs. The fact is, we'd taken six wickets and given ourselves a genuine chance of taking this match by the scruff of the neck. Bring on Day 2!

Despite his poor bowling performance, I still made a point after lunch of offering a few encouraging words to Mitch – which hopefully made up for the string of less than encouraging ones I directed at him during the morning session.

Australian Cricket Team – Tour Rules

1. <u>CURFEW and ALCOHOL</u>
a. Curfew is 12 midnight in the hotel
b. No alcohol the day before a Test match
c. No alcohol during a Test match
d. Curfew and drinking rule may be
varied after a win

2. <u>CLOTHING</u>
a. Team shirt to all team meetings
b. Team shirt and dress shorts/tracksuit
pants on bus to all matches
c. Correct training attire to be worn at all
team training sessions

3. <u>PUNCTUALITY</u>
a. All players to be on bus prior to
designated departure time
b. All players to be at breakfast 20
minutes prior to designated time of
departure — NO EXEMPTIONS!
c. Captain exempted from Rule 3(b)
d. All players to be at team meetings prior
to designated time of meeting

4. <u>MEETINGS</u>
a. Attendance compulsory
b. No iPods!
c. No leaving until Vinny finished speaking
d. Wives/partners welcome to attend but
not to speak

Meeting the Queen at Lords is always a highlight of any Ashes tour. On this occasion all the boys were pretty pumped up; clean shaven, hair combed, a couple had even used deodorant. Mind you, this was nothing compared to Vinny who had a bloody suit and tie on! We lined up in the middle of the ground and waited for ages as Her Maj worked her way along the line of players, starting with the Poms (who must have won the toss) before moving on to us. We had all been instructed to bow slightly which is something we're quite used to doing, as it's generally required whenever a selector enters the Australian dressing room. Although Huss obviously got a little flustered and ended up doing what appeared to be a cross between a curtsy and ducking a short-pitched ball. Royal officials had briefed us all on the rules. When first addressing the Queen we were told to use the expression 'Your Majesty'. Should the conversation continue (and it rarely does) you can then say 'Ma'am'. If you get to 'Liz' then things have probably gone too far. To be safe, we were all told to say nothing more than 'Pleased to meet you, Ma'am'. Various minders hovered about nervously, hardly surprising given some of the well-documented incidents involving previous Aussie teams. In 1977 Dennis Lillee famously breached royal protocol by holding out a pen and paper and asking Her Majesty for her autograph. A similar faux pas took place in 2005 when Warnie also produced a pen and paper, this time asking the Queen if she'd like his autograph.

For tour matches we sometimes relax our normally strict dietary standards. After all, there's only so many energy bars you can eat.

There are some moments on a long tour when you just have to take a break from cricket, to switch the brain into neutral and relax. Choosing to do so while fielding at second slip this morning was, in hindsight, a mistake and Sidds still hasn't forgiven me for grassing an edge from his second delivery.

Going in to bat

Equipment sponsorship is very important for players, and it's an area I find particularly interesting. I switched from Gunn & Moore to Gray-Nicholls because they gave me input into some of their designs, only to switch back when Gray-Nicholls ceased production of my revolutionary silicon-centred blade.

Truth is, the best bats in the world are made by England's Millichamp & Hall. Pretty much all the guys use them, and those of us who are sponsored by other bat manufacturers simply put our sponsor's stickers over the top. Once during a Test match in South Africa I was forced to 'retire hurt' when one of my stickers began to peel off.

Out on a cricket field you are surrounded, not just by eager-eyed fans but by hundreds of cameras waiting to pick up your every reaction. That's why, no matter how angry I might be at getting out cheaply or being on the end of a bad decision, I'm careful to control my emotions. Let's face it, Warwick Todd is a role model, an icon (and, in some states of Australia, a registered company), so I have to be careful to set a good example. I've only ever sworn out loud once on a cricket field, an incident that received a lot of coverage because it was at Lords and I was being introduced to the Queen at the time. Since then, I've kept my mouth shut until back in the rooms. Then you can really let fly.

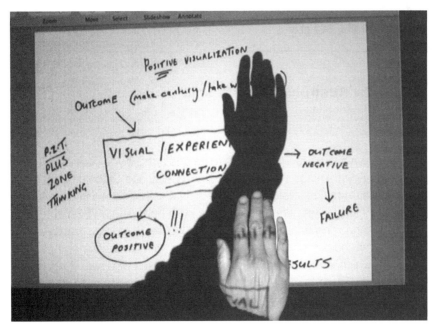

Sidds interrupts our sports psychologist's presentation to ask whether he's still allowed to bowl bouncers.

There's only one thing worse than a long team meeting, and that's no one letting you know that it's over.

17 Friday

England v Australia (Second Test)
Lords
Day 2

Well, it's been a long day. Nine hours (nine and a half if you count the match referee hearing). Things started really well as Hilfy and Sidds ploughed through the Poms' middle order. But then, just as happened in Cardiff, England's 10th wicket partnership dug in, with Anderson and Onions adding 47 annoying runs. To make matters worse, Sidds had to leave the ground after chucking up on the hallowed turf (at least he managed to hit the pitch, which is more than could be said for Mitch who was spraying the ball everywhere) and we found ourselves struggling to wrap up the innings. Anderson had a life on 5 when BJ failed to move across and hold onto a regulation catch; our keeper claimed later that his feet had become stuck in some of Punter's discarded chewing gum. Eventually Mitch took this last wicket, meaning the Poms ended up with a total of 425.

Our innings was almost derailed early on by some terrible umpiring decisions. Now, before I go into details, let me say this. I think the vast majority of international umpires are very good at what they do. (A list of exceptions can be found on my website; click on 'Koertzen' and follow the links.) But what we suffered today was simply unacceptable. First up, Boof was given out on just 4, caught behind to a ball he didn't remotely get a bat on. Then, a few overs later, Punter was the victim of a slips catch that clearly didn't carry. Of course, this didn't stop the Poms all appealing and, after conferring with each other, the umpires ruled that our skipper was indeed out. Now I know the issue of disputed catches has always created problems and, while some favour the increased use of technology, I propose a better system, based on trust and mutual respect. Put simply, if we take a catch and the fielder involved believes it carried then his word should be accepted. And, similarly, if an English player takes a catch and he thinks it carried, then we should go to the TV replay.

Luckily Katto and Huss were able to hold out for the next few overs and we went to lunch on 2/22.

During lunch we were officially presented to the Queen and Prince Philip. As usual an aide ran through the basic rules on how to address them, telling us 'it's Ma'am as in farm' at which point I added 'and Phil as in dill'! Not sure this bloke had much of a sense of humour, which could perhaps explain why I was pushed towards the back of the receiving party. Mind you, Sidds missed out altogether as he was still suffering the effects of food poisoning and it was felt that chucking on Her Majesty might constitute a breach of royal protocol. I have, of course, met the Queen before and she's really quite nice. She reminds me of my grandmother a bit, only without the smell or temper.

I tell you what, the next session of play was pretty nerve-racking, watching on as Katto, Huss and then Pup tried to slowly build a total. People often ask me what goes on in the rooms when we're waiting for our turn to bat. The truth is, it's different for each player. Some of the guys like to pace about, others sit quietly watching the play. The next batsman in is always looked after. If he wants a drink or the music turned up, or to sit in a particular spot, it's his for the asking. During particularly tense passages of play a shoulder rub is not out of the question.

When Huss went for a well-compiled 51 it was time for Yours Truly to step onto the hallowed turf. As always, I paused for final checks: thigh pad, inner thigh guard, arm guard, chest guard, nicotine patch. Check. Now to make that famous trip from dressing room to ground. Out the back door, down three flights of stairs to the Long Room, walk into the kitchen and realise you've gone one flight too many, back upstairs, through the Long Room, smiling at the members in their egg and bacon ties, quick photo with a potential footwear sponsor and then down those three steps to the playing surface.

I'm a confidence player and for me the most important thing to do at the start of an innings is relieve the pressure by getting a few early runs. And I tell you what, there's nothing quite like the sound of a ball hitting the middle. Unless it's middle stump, in which case it's the worst sound in the world. Unfortunately, that's exactly what happened to me, bowled by Anderson going for a lofted hoik over mid-on. My dismissal led to something of a mini-collapse and we were 8/152 by the time play was stopped at 6.23 pm due to bad light. It should, by rights, have been stopped earlier due to bad umpiring but you won't hear us complaining. We know we've got a big job ahead of us, still requiring a further 74 runs just to avoid the follow-on. But a very wise man once said 'the toughest challenges in life can only be met head on'. I think it was either Confucius or Justin Langer, but either way, I agree. This match is not over yet.

July

18 Saturday

England v Australia (Second Test)
Lords
Day 3

Predictably enough the press all got stuck into our performance yesterday, saying that Australia's middle order 'threw away' their wickets with 'misjudged, reckless strokes'. P. Roebuck took specific aim at me, calling my innings 'profligate'. All I can say is that if you're going to bag someone at least have the courtesy to do it in plain English.

It was a fairly sombre ride to the ground this morning, with everyone aware that we are batting to defend Australia's 75-year record of being unbeaten at Lords. In these tight moments it's vital to stay positive and our keeper, BJ, often has the knack of coming up with the right words at the right time. This morning he was straight to the point. 'We're f*#ked.'

Haurie and Sidds held out for a 44-run partnership, a pretty gutsy effort when you realise that Ritzy was batting with a dislocated finger. But I guess that's a hallmark of Aussie players. When blokes like (South Africa's) Graeme Smith refuse to even take the field because of a broken finger we push on. I've seen Sidds bowl with a busted foot. When I was hospitalised in India with dysentery I got out of bed and batted during the second innings, even though I required a runner to carry my drip. (Actually, two runners – the other was carrying a bed-pan.) That's guts. And that's what we showed today. Unfortunately, it was not quite enough and we fell short of the follow-on target, being dismissed for 215.

England decided not to enforce the follow-on and continued their fine batting form, with all of the top order getting good starts except for Bopara whose innings was most definitely profligate. Meanwhile, our bowlers continued to struggle, with both Hilfy and Sidds going wicketless; although Haurie extracted some good turn from the pitch, picking up three wickets. Mitch bowled with quite a bit of variation, sending down some loose balls as well as some really loose ones.

The day was not free of controversy, with – surprise, surprise – Rudi Koertzen at its centre. Haurie took a great catch to dismiss Ravi Bopara, only to see Koertzen decide to refer it to the third umpire who, in turn, decided it hadn't carried. Now this was offensive on several grounds. For a start, not trusting the word of an AUSTRALIAN cricketer. Listen, I know Haurie and I know that he plays the game hard but he plays it fair. And if that ball had hit the ground then he would have said so. Maybe not on the spot, or during the course of the series, but it would eventually creep out in a newspaper column or biography. That's the kind of bloke he is. Secondly, where was the third umpire two days ago when Punter was given out? Our skipper was understandably not happy with this sort of inconsistency and took the opportunity to confront umpire Koertzen and Pietersen, the non-striker, leading to an awkward moment that could easily have escalated into violence, which would have been a real pity on this MCC-designated 'spirit of cricket day'.

Rain eventually ended play in the 72nd over with England sitting on 6/311, a 521-run lead. More famous faces were spotted in the crowd today, including Michael Parkinson, Rolf Harris and Mick Jagger, who were all taking advantage of the Over 65 discounted ticket offer. Also watching was former Australian prime minister John Howard, a self-confessed cricket tragic. Punter invited him into the dressing room during the luncheon interval. I suspect he was a little disappointed that none of us were there at the time, but I believe he spoke with a few of our room attendants.

In hindsight, my victory celebrations on Day 3 may have been just a touch premature.

July

19 Sunday

England v Australia (Second Test)
Lords
Day 4

Heavy rain overnight threatened to prevent play today but, thanks to the state-of-the-art drainage system here at Lords, we were able to get away just 15 minutes late. Before the start of play we lined up in the middle for another team photo. We had, of course, taken one on the first day and the official reason given for this re-shoot was 'lighting issues', although there's a strong rumour going round that one of our higher profile batsmen may have revealed more than just his teeth. Normally these sorts of deliberate 'wardrobe malfunctions' are picked up by our media people but somehow this one must have snuck past.

England declared on their overnight score meaning we were chasing a formidable total of 522 runs for victory. Lesser teams might have been overwhelmed by a figure such as this but it's simply not the Aussie way to give up. An old coach of mine, Ken Pike, used to say 'only losers lose hope'. And, despite his unexpected suicide a few years later, I've never forgotten that simple message.

In summary, it was an excellent day of Test cricket, sadly marred by some less-than-excellent umpiring decisions. First up, Katto was given out by Rudi Koertzen to an obvious no-ball from Flintoff. Then, a few overs later, Boof edged one from Flintoff to first slip where Strauss claimed the catch 'low down' (i.e. after it had bounced). Punter, who was watching from the other end, rightly told Boof to stand his ground but umpire Koertzen refused to call for a TV replay and sent our opener on his way. To top things off, Huss was then also given out – 'caught' at first slip to a ball he didn't even make contact with. By this stage the mood in the rooms was getting a little 'tense' to say the least. And Flintoff was bowling particularly well. However, there's an old saying in cricket that a batsman should play the ball, not the bowler, meaning that you should focus on the ball itself rather than the person who is bowling it. (I think I may have over-explained that.) Anyway, I knew that it was time for someone to stand up and be counted. In pressure situations such as this I believe strongly in taking the fight up to the opposition. If you walk out there looking defeated and immediately go on the defensive, this sends the wrong message.

My approach is to get on the front foot and show the bowler who's boss with aggressive strokeplay. Yes, in hindsight a one-handed reverse sweep just before tea may not have been the wisest choice of shot but I was trying to shake things up a little. And it almost came off, it was just sheer bad luck that they happened to have a man fielding in that position (the wicket-keeper) who took the catch.

Luckily Pup and BJ were able to steady the ship with some inspired batting that saw our vice-captain reach his century in near even-time. As usual Pup was pretty pumped up and celebrated his 11th Test century with a customary kiss of the helmet and a wave to one of his key sponsors. By the end of play he had made it to 125 and, whether we win or not, this will go down as one of Australian cricket's finest innings. I guess there have been a few: Dean Jones making 210 in Madras back in '96; Tugga silencing his critics with a near perfect century in the fading light of a Sydney Test; and, dare I suggest, the explosive 127 in 112 balls I scored back in 2005. Sure, some knockers have said 'it was only against Kenya' but I think this misses the point. Anyway, Pup played an inspired knock and, together with BJ, produced an unbeaten stand of 185, giving us a real chance of saving the match.

It's hard to describe the mood in our dressing room after play. We know there's a mountain still to climb. At 5/313 we still need another 209 runs for victory but, with Pup and BJ showing true Aussie grit, anything's possible. And, as Punter said back at the hotel, 'we simply have to back ourselves'. (Although, at odds of 2/1, I couldn't quite see the value in this bet.) After dinner we broke into two groups: those who need to bat tomorrow (who had an early night) and the rest of us (who didn't).

Tonight I decided to come up with a new set of '10 Commandments', Todd style. Here's what I wrote.

1. Enjoy your cricket.
2. Always give 100%, if not 110% but no more without medical supervision.
3. Learn from your mistakes.
4. Be competitive: hard but fair.
5. Perseverance is the key; there's no room for quitters.
6. I'll finish points 6-10 tomorrow.

20 Monday

England v Australia (Second Test)
Lords
Day 5

If anyone thought this Test match was all over, then they obviously didn't tell the English fans. Lords was completely sold out for a fifth day running and the sound as we arrived at the ground was simply deafening. I guess the Poms were sensing victory, and that's something they don't get to experience very often.

Before he went out to bat our wicket-keeper looked at us all in the eye, saying, 'There isn't a single person out there who thinks we can win this game.' Gritting his teeth, he lowered his voice and said, 'Let's just see about that.' With those words, he grabbed his bat and walked out to take strike. It was a truly spine-tingling moment, in no way diminished by the fact he was back in the rooms two overs later, caught behind without adding to his overnight score. BJ *believed* we could win, and that was enough.

Unfortunately Pup also went a few overs later for 136 and from there the rot set in, with Ritzy and Sidds going cheaply. After each of these wickets Flintoff the destroyer would celebrate in customary fashion, by punching the air and having another injection in his knee. Mitch batted well but couldn't quite hold out until lunch, losing his wicket with the total on 406, still 115 runs short. Naturally the crowd went ballistic, as did the England players who immediately formed a celebratory huddle. Now I'm all for back-slapping, high-fives and even the occasional pat on the bum, but if you ask me the sort of extended man-hugging they displayed really crossed the line.

Flintoff was named Man of the Match, a pretty fair call as he was England's most valuable contributor, although umpire Rudi Koertzen would surely come a close second. Watching on while another side accepts the winner's trophy is never easy but we managed to do it with good grace and a minimum of eye-rolling. Punter spoke well, acknowledging that England were the better side and congratulating them on a fine victory. A few people later commented about our skipper's three-day growth and the fact it shows he's been under great pressure. Let me tell you right here, there was nothing 'three day' about that beard; Punter hasn't shaved since May.

Understandably, the boys were all pretty shattered in the dressing room as we dissected the Test over a few quiet beers. The knowledge that we have allowed Australia's 75-year unbeaten run at Lords to be broken was pretty hard to take. But in these moments it's always important to focus on the positives and we toasted Pup's big innings. His name was now up on the board for Test centuries at Lords. We also realised we had an afternoon off – there was another positive worth toasting. After a few hours we were joined by the wives and partners. It was good having the girls there as they were able to sympathise with our loss, and help clean up some of the broken glasses.

Sitting in my room just before midnight, the reality of today's defeat finally began to sink in. The fact we are now 1-0 down and fighting to save the series – it's a position I don't like being in. I'll be honest, losing the Ashes in 2005 ranks as one of the lowest points of my cricketing career, second only to the misguided alcohol ban imposed during our 1999 tour of the West Indies. It was shortly after that history-making defeat when the name W. Todd was first seriously thrown into the ring as a potential replacement for Punter as captain. Now I won't lie, it's something I have thought about from time to time. Actually, a lot. The privilege of leading Australia into battle would be an enormous honour and I would love to one day captain this great country. Or any country for that matter, I'm open to offers.

There's a clear difference between manly celebration and inappropriate contact. This sort of heated fondling has no place on a sporting field.

July

21 Tuesday

London

Not surprisingly, the local press have had a field day with our loss at
Lords and the usual series of mindless headlines ('Fred turns the Aussies
to Ashes') greeted us all at breakfast. Of course, it's easy for blokes
like Katto, Snorks and BJ who have a strict policy not to read any press
articles when on tour. Others, like Sidds and Hilfy, can't actually read
so it's even easier for them. I make a point of at least glancing through
the newspaper on the off-chance there's something useful I might take
away, but that's fairly rare. The British press, in particular, is largely made
up of tragic ex-players turned columnists who think their opinions on the
modern game are somehow still relevant. Honestly, why anyone would
care about the rantings of some sad, superannuated fool who is still
pining for starched collars and eight-ball overs has got me beat. While
you kind of expect old opponents like Mike Atherton or Geoffrey Boycott
to have a go at you on TV, it can really hurt to hear that ex-team-mates
are also on the attack. Word has filtered through from home that SBS
TV anchors Stuart McGill and Greg 'Mo' Matthews have both been quite
critical of our form so far. There is, of course, an old saying about this: no
one's ever made a mistake in the commentary box. (Which, technically,
is not true. In 2007 I was doing special comments for Fox Sports and
made the mistake of calling our executive producer a 'f#*king dickhead'.
I didn't realise he was watching.) Mind you, this criticism hasn't just been
confined to ex-players. We heard today that Russell Crowe had a crack
at us on the BBC for being 'weak'! When I think of the times we've put
up with that bloke in the dressing rooms. And not just him – we had to
play one of his songs on the team music box. Anyway, let them try and
write us off! The Australian team is full of men with courage, commitment
and a never-say-die attitude, and I know we'll bounce back from this
situation. But we've certainly got some work to do.

Injury-wise, things are not looking good. Quite a few of the boys are
nursing either bruises, sprains, strains or serious hangovers. One of the
worst affected is Punter who was hit on the finger by a short ball from
Anderson during the second innings. Our skipper rarely shows pain (in
fact, the only time I've seen him actually cry is watching the greyhounds)
but he was clearly in agony on the field and his finger is still sore. But
without doubt our biggest concern would have to be Mitch. He's gone

from being Australia's number one strike bowler in South Africa to a shadow of his former self. He spent this morning working in the nets with bowling coach Troy Cooley and, from what I could see, seemed to be regaining a bit of rhythm, thanks to Cool's guidance and the electrodes attached to his pants.

If you ask me, Mitch is simply going through a bit of a form slump. It's something that happens to all players at one stage or another and is often related to a loss of confidence. Whenever I've started doubting myself over the years I've always found it useful to go back and look at footage of myself during the good times: big innings, collecting Man of the Match awards, my guest appearance on *Celebrity Dog School* – these sort of career highlights can only serve to lift your spirits. There's no doubting it, Mitch is a confidence player who needs to believe in himself, even if the rest of us are struggling to do so.

The other worry is Boof, our young star who is also yet to really find form on this tour. There's some talk of Shane Watson stepping into the opener's role but, to me, this would be a dicey move. Despite playing a lot of matches, Watto's experience of going in first is pretty much limited to one-day cricket and the luncheon buffet queue.

Fortunately these sorts of issues can wait for a bit as the rest of us were given the next two days off. A bunch of players – Katto, Snorks, BJ, Ronnie, Hilfy and myself – decided to do a bit of sightseeing. We took a double-decker bus tour and ended up at the London Eye, which was good but a bit slow. Hilfy actually fell asleep halfway up and missed some of the more spectacular sights. After that we took a boat tour of the Thames, checked out Buckingham Palace and did a bit of shopping. We then decided to see a West End show but most of them were either booked out or crap. In the end we got 'restricted view' tickets to *Dirty Dancing* which meant we didn't get to see any of the dirty bits, just a lot of dancing. After that we hit the clubs and enjoyed a few more quiet drinks. It was a great day, one on which we were able to relax and forget about cricket, and the second Test loss and all the crap being written about us. It was then we realised we'd also forgotten about Hilfy – he was still on the London Eye and, by the time we got back to him, was going round for the 53rd time.

July

22 Wednesday

London

I was woken this morning by a phone call informing me that former Australian captain and Channel 9 commentary legend Richie Benaud had been killed in a tragic accident at his French vineyard. Turned out to be a 'Gotcha Call' from some pathetic FM radio breakfast show in Brisbane. Look, I love a laugh as much as the next bloke (who was the person who filled Pup's protector with Dencorub?) but this was taking things too far.

As it happens, I was not the only member of the squad less than happy this morning. One of our junior members (who shall remain nameless for obvious reasons) apparently hooked up with a female 'fan' a couple of days back and, according to the boys, they spent a pretty steamy night back here at the team hotel. When she left the next morning he told her to give him a call but, several days later, his phone is yet to ring. Turns out it's been stolen, along with some of his credit cards and a signed bat. There's a lesson there.

More negative articles today attacking our performance at Lords and questioning the team's chances of retaining the Ashes. I don't mind this sort of crap from the local press, but when ex-Aussie players decide to put the boot in it can really hurt. Listen Deano, you're a decent bloke and a good mate, but you're wrong about this squad 'lacking commitment'. We are completely focused on winning this series and will not rest until that (replica) urn is safely back in Australia.

The other big news this morning was that England's Kevin Pietersen is out for the rest of the Ashes series with an Achilles tendon injury. While I'm not all that upset (Pietersen is the sort of player that can really ignite a side) this sort of thing does remind you just how fragile we elite cricketers are. We've had Bing and Watto both miss games through strains; they've got Flintoff on one good leg and now Pietersen out for good. I guess I've been pretty fortunate with injuries over the years. Sure, there's been the usual knee twangs and groin twinges but nothing too serious. The longest I've been kept off the park was 2004 when I had an operation on my wrist where they took out a piece of floating bone. My surgeon was quite surprised at the time as the bone in question turned out not to be my own. But I was out of plaster and back on the ground within six weeks. I've known blokes who have missed entire seasons with injury.

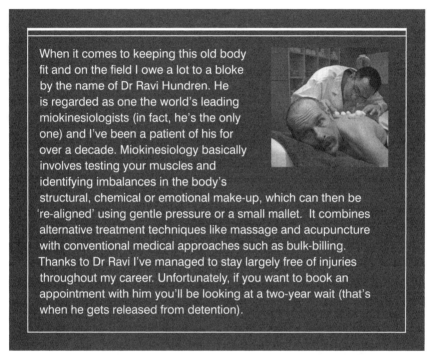

When it comes to keeping this old body fit and on the field I owe a lot to a bloke by the name of Dr Ravi Hundren. He is regarded as one the world's leading miokinesiologists (in fact, he's the only one) and I've been a patient of his for over a decade. Miokinesiology basically involves testing your muscles and identifying imbalances in the body's structural, chemical or emotional make-up, which can then be 're-aligned' using gentle pressure or a small mallet. It combines alternative treatment techniques like massage and acupuncture with conventional medical approaches such as bulk-billing. Thanks to Dr Ravi I've managed to stay largely free of injuries throughout my career. Unfortunately, if you want to book an appointment with him you'll be looking at a two-year wait (that's when he gets released from detention).

After breakfast we travelled by coach to Northampton. We spend a lot of time on the team bus but it's not a problem as there's always something to do, whether it's enjoying DVDs, playing cards, listening to music or just watching our physio work on Watto's various injuries. Punter, Pup and BJ stayed behind in London as they will be rested for the next tour match, in order to give Sarfraz, Watto and Ronnie a chance to show their stuff. Huss will act as captain. The rest of us will act impressed.

At the team meeting this afternoon we discussed security, or the lack of it, at grounds where we are playing. Already on this tour we have had bags and equipment stolen and at Hove, during our tour match, a streaker managed to get onto the ground and run amongst the players. The fact he turned out to be a former Victorian Shield player over here on holiday does not diminish the danger posed by this lax approach to player safety. Team manager Steve Bernard has promised to find someone (else) to look into it.

July

23 Thursday

Northampton

Up early this morning for another big training session. After the luxury of Lords, facilities here at Northampton's ground are a little less luxurious. The lockers are small, most of the showers luke-warm and Pup can't find anywhere in the bathroom to plug his hairdryer in. Even so, we pushed on.

Following a good hit-out in the nets this morning we were joined over lunch by a guest speaker, the UK-based sports psychologist Malcolm Bonn. Inviting a range of experts in to address the team is quite customary on long tours such as this and a good way to inspire the boys. Malcolm gave a fairly passionate speech about the importance of enjoying our time at the top, telling us that, before we knew it, we'd be dropped or forced to retire through injury and then the money and fame would disappear; not to mention the former team-mates we thought were friends but now don't want to know us, as we all faced up to life without cricket, often doing a job we hated if we were lucky enough to get a job at all. By the time he had finished we were all too depressed to continue training.

Still a lot of talk that Watto may be called up to step into the opener's position if Boof fails in tomorrow's tour match. He's apparently recovered from his thigh injury and is keen to give the top spot a crack. Don't get me wrong, Watto would be great. In fact, he used to open for Queensland a few years back when Lang retired and just because the experiment was a *complete failure* should in no way affect the selector's thinking. That said, I would also be happy to be considered should Boofa continue to

Technology – Toddy's Take

I'm all for technology, provided it leads to results out on the paddock. And I accept that there's a place for video analysis in a team meeting, examining footage of players in the nets or at the crease as a means of identifying potential weaknesses in technique. But calling the boys together last night in order to watch security camera footage of me outside a Northampton nightclub is simply an abuse of this facility.

struggle. Speaking of struggling, we're also still getting a lot of questions about Mitch and his apparent form slump. The official line is that Mitch is still one of our strike bowlers and a valuable part of the Australian team. As I said to one journo, he can still bowl with good pace and accuracy. Unfortunately, just not at the same time.

There's been a lot of continued speculation from commentators about why we lost the Second Test with some questioning whether this Australian line-up has lost its 'mojo'; that special killer quality that makes a team great. As usual, there's a lot of crap being written, but I do have a theory. And it's nothing to do with loose deliveries or rash strokeplay. It's something far more fundamental. Hair. Interesting fact: this is the first Australian team to tour England without any player sporting serious facial cover. (And I don't count a three-day growth, that's not commitment.) The reason is, of course, that too many of the boys have signed deals with Gillette or other razor companies as part of which they've got to walk around clean shaven or they cop a fine. In my day the Leadership Group would never have allowed something like this. Come to think of it, we would never have allowed a Leadership Group. The bottom line is: beards, 'taches and big sidies are what made the Aussie squad great. Past teams didn't worry about grooming or aftershave. Back then you could get dropped simply for being found in possession of a comb.

We opted not to have a team meeting this evening. Instead we just got together at the bar for a chat about tomorrow's game and a few fitness issues, at which point we realised we were having a meeting.

News that a local nightclub was offering free drink cards to any Australian player who turned up in Test gear prompted an immediate response from the guys.

July

24 Friday

Australia v Northamptonshire (Tour match)
Northampton
Day 1

As usual, the final make-up of the team was not decided until after warm-ups this morning. As I was getting my eye in with a few throw-downs in the nets, I glanced across the ground to where Watto was undergoing a final fitness test. It was hard to tell how it was going for the big Queenslander, but the sight of our physio, two stretcher attendants and an ambulance standing by didn't exactly fill us with confidence.

Speaking of teams, there was disappointing news that Northamptonshire have chosen to withdraw several of their better players for this match, including South Africans Andrew Hall and Johan van der Wath. (I had a couple of offensive Afrikaan expressions I was keen to road test – no point doing it on a local.) Meanwhile Monty Panesar is being 'rested', which makes bugger-all sense as the bloke didn't even play at Lords. What's he being rested from? Life?

Fielding over here in slip you've got as much chance of catching the flu as you have of picking up a wicket.

Talk about cold. Despite thermal underwear, a singlet, sleeveless vest and jumper I was still freezing today, with the wind cutting through us all during warm-ups. And this is supposed to be summer! Eventually the clouds lifted and a weak sun poked through, at which point some of the local team started calling for ice vests.

Boof began the day with a firmly struck cover drive to the boundary but fell soon after to another short-of-a-length delivery, fending a ball to gully for just 10 runs. I tell you what, it was a long walk back to the rooms for our embattled opener, made longer by Punter insisting that we lock the doors and force him to wait outside next to the bus. Katto then went for 25, giving Watto a chance to show us his form, which he duly did, belting 84 runs from just 96 deliveries, including 15 boundaries and a six.

I came in with the score on 145, determined to put the indifferent form of Lords behind me. Whenever things are not going all that well at the crease I'll make a point of returning to the basics. Taking guard I clear my head of all distractions and simply try to focus by asking myself a series of questions: Am I watching the ball? Am I moving my feet? Is my back lift okay? Should I have said 'yes' to that Gatorade offer despite their refusal to cover travel expenses? Before you know it, I am back 'in the zone' and playing decent cricket. It certainly worked for me today as I got off to a good start, really middling the ball and working it to all parts of the ground. By this stage I was batting with Huss, which can be hard work; not only are there constant mid-pitch conferences, he's always looking for that extra run. Conversations tend to go like this:

Huss: Yes! Yes! Yes! Yesyesyesyesyesyesyesyesyessss!
Todd: No.
Huss: There was two in it!
Todd: It's a f*#king drinks break Huss.
Huss: Sure.

Unfortunately play was interrupted three times by rain but we still managed to take the score along to 3/231 before bad light ended proceedings. I'm feeling good and believe I can use this opportunity to re-build confidence with a really decent score. Of course, I'm not going to dwell on this; getting ahead of yourself is exactly what I did during my last innings and it's a mistake I don't intend to repeat.

July

25 Saturday

Australia v Northamptonshire (Tour match)
Northampton
Day 2

Okay, I repeated it. I was on 46, thinking how just one boundary would give me a half-century, when I failed to pick a slower delivery from Lucas and was trapped leg-before. Honestly, I could have kicked myself but, instead, kicked the stumps, before making that long walk back to the rooms. Fortunately most of our middle order got good starts, including Huss who went on to post a solid 75 before retiring to 'give some of the other guys a turn at the crease'. Wish I'd thought of that excuse.

We declared on 8/308 and the Northants guys started their second innings. For the first time on this tour, Mitch was not given the new ball, only coming on after Sidds and Sarfraz had opened the attack. Even in the field his woes continued, dropping an easy catch off Sarfraz. Fortunately Sarfraz bounced back, teaming up with Watto to pick up some valuable wickets. When Mitch was eventually thrown the ball (which he then dropped) we had to endure another less than excellent spell, with our former pace spearhead straying too short and conceding runs at around 6 per over. Irish import Niall O'Brien was his chief tormentor, smashing Mitch to all parts of the ground. I was fielding in close for much of this innings and, despite wearing a helmet and pads, copped quite a few nasty blows and near misses. In an effort to unsettle the batsman I strolled up to him after one over and said, 'You boys want to play it tough do you?' O'Brien said, 'Like we always do' but I thought he said, 'You bet we do'; so I then added, 'Well let's see how you like a taste of your own medicine', but he thought I said, 'Well let's bring it on again then', so he said, 'Okay', only I thought he said, 'No way', at which point I realised it's almost pointless trying to maintain a serious sledging conversation when you've both got tight helmets blocking your ears.

Northamptonshire declared on 7/226, giving us a day and a half to chase down the total. Boof managed a pressure-relieving half-century, but it was not the most convincing of knocks. He opened with Ronnie who looked far more settled, ending the day unbeaten on 69. I was unlucky not to score a hundred, falling to a catch on the boundary just 98 runs short.

Back at the hotel I received a phone call from the sports editor of *The Australian*, saying that there was a problem with my latest column and that someone was threatening to sue for defamation. I thought this was odd as we normally employ a high-profile lawyer to proofread my columns to check for any potential problems. Turns out this lawyer is the bloke who is threatening to sue.

Then it was time to do my regular cross back to B107 FM on the Gold Coast. As their 'official Ashes correspondent' all I have to do is phone up once a week and file a report for their breakfast show. But when I got through to the producer he (or she, it's hard to tell) told me that I'm no longer required. I naturally asked, 'Why?' and he (or she) said there was a problem with my last cross. The transcript only just arrived:

BROADCAST MONITORS

Transcript

Station:	**B107 FM**	Date:	**18/07/09**
Program:	**THE BIG BREAKFAST**	Time:	**8.07 AM**
Compere:	**DAVE ADDISON AND MARIE CLODE**		
Item:	**INTERVIEW WITH REGULAR CRICKET CORRESPONDENT WARWICK TODD REPORTING FROM 2009 ASHES TOUR.**		

HOST: That's coming up in the next hour, but right now, all the way from London, it's the man himself, Warwick Todd. How's it going Toddy?

TODD: G'day mate.

HOST 2: Hi Warwick, it's Marie here.

TODD: G'day mate.

HOST: Now, talk about excitement, this Test match has had it all. What's the mood like in the Aussie dressing room?

TODD: It's good mate. It's, you know, the boys are a little, um, you know, (INAUDIBLE) pretty pumped, I think, um, oh f—k it, can we start again? Take 2?

HOST: No.

TODD: Why not?

HOST: This is live.

TODD: (INAUDIBLE)

July

26 Sunday

Australia v Northamptonshire (Tour match)
Northampton
Day 3

At 6.30 am my mobile phone began running hot with calls – not exactly the start you want on a match day. Turned out *Inside Cricket* magazine had just published its 'Team of the Century' and Yours Truly was apparently in the squad. Really, I've got to laugh. While these sort of 'best ever' lists and 'top ten' rankings generate a lot of public interest, they really don't mean a thing to us players. I honestly couldn't tell you whether I made *Wisden*'s 2005 'Super Squad'* or why I missed out on being included in ABC *Grandstand*'s 'All Australia XI'.** I play for Australia and that's all that matters. If other experts think I deserve a place in some sort of 'All Time XI'*** then that's up to them.

We pushed on this morning to reach 270 runs before declaring and giving the local team another chance to bat. Ronnie was our star with the ball, taking four wickets (to add to his impressive run total of 32 and 75). Not bad for a bloke whose only involvement in the tour so far has been net sessions and taking Punter's clothes to the laundromat. Mitch continued to be a little expensive but did manage to finally pick up a wicket, albeit that of their tail-ender who may have simply lost sight of the ball in the drizzle. Debate continues to rage as to whether he can fully regain his form in time for the Third Test but, if you ask me, I think Mitch still has a very real place in our squad. As a net bowler. I was pleased with my performance in the field. Not only did I take a catch, I was able to cut off a boundary with a spectacular slide into an advertising hoarding belonging to one of my local sponsors that should, hopefully, get them some decent TV coverage.

Thanks to an improved bowling effort we had little trouble dismissing Northamptonshire for 217 runs, giving us our first victory since knocking off New Zealand in a T20 practice match back in June. Not only that, it was our maiden first-class victory of the tour! While *technically* the team song can only be sung after Test wins, it was agreed to let us belt out a few verses and we stayed at the ground celebrating 'til about midnight. The following Tuesday.

* I did
** Because the selection panel was biased against left-handers
*** I do

A close call

When Pup and Katto got into a fight over the singing of our team song last year it made the headlines. But believe it or not, this was not the first time the team song has nearly led to violence. After defeating Sri Lanka in the 2007 World Cup final in Barbados we naturally celebrated long and hard. Around about 11.00 pm we left the rooms and headed out onto the field to sing the team song. All of a sudden a couple of West Indian security guards came over and told us to clear off. We tried explaining how important it was that we sing the song but they wouldn't listen. One of them even grabbed Punter. I'm telling you, touching the Australian captain is simply something you don't do (even his wife Rianna has to get written permission from Cricket Australia) and things very nearly turned ugly. In the end we were forced back into the rooms where our singing duties were duly completed.

July

27 Monday

I have no recollection of this day. Despite catching a few glimpses of myself on CCTV cameras, it's a complete blur. I don't know where we went, what I did or how I got the tattoo 'I ♥ Denise' on my left thigh. Top day.

28 Tuesday

Birmingham

We travelled north this morning to Birmingham, the venue for the Third Test. As usual, most of us took the opportunity to rest up, watch DVDs or play cards. A few of the boys like to relax with a book, although, to tell the truth, I'm not a great reader. I struggle to get through the newspaper and as for novels, forget it. About the only thing I tend to read on tour are cricket magazines and prepared statements of apology. With the Edgbaston Test just a few days away, our biggest worry continues to be injuries. We've got Bing, Watto, Choco and Pup all under a serious fitness cloud. On the plus side, because of their various conditions we got to leave the bus in the hotel's disabled parking spot.

A question I'm often asked by fans is 'what exactly goes on in the lead-up to a big match?' Obviously the answer depends on where you're playing, but here in England there's a fairly set pattern. A few days out we check into the team hotel. I like to unpack my bags, hang up my shirts and training gear and set out a few ashtrays so it feels like home. We then have a full-on training session at the ground where I prefer to work on match-specific movements. For example, today I practised running between wickets, appealing and send-offs. Afterwards we'll have a recovery session, which can consist of a swim or a massage, maybe both. The next few days tend to fly by in a whirl of training, workouts, the inevitable signing sessions and meetings with official team sponsors. The day before a Test is often my favourite as all activities are completely optional. And this is where you start to see differences in the way players go about preparing. Some blokes I've played with, like Haydos or Pigeon, used to go right away from the action. Maybe sightseeing or catching up with friends. Warnie once went to New York (only just making it back for the toss). On this tour Bing likes to hang out at the hotel and play his guitar to anyone interested in listening, meaning he often spends the day alone.

A training session at the ground was scheduled for this afternoon but due to recent rain the outfield was completely soaked, so we headed back to the hotel bar where several of the boys were hoping to achieve a similar state. But Punter put a stop to this, ordering a match planning session. Before any big game we meet for a planning session, usually hosted by the Plan and Theme team. This Test's theme is Intent and Intimidate. Katto started off by playing a highlights video of our recent victory over South

Africa that really got the boys fired up, as did BJ's tape choice, *Girls of the Playboy Mansion*. Unfortunately, Punter made us turn it off halfway through so we could concentrate on the upcoming match.

While team meetings obviously play a valuable role in preparing for a game, in my opinion they do tend to go on a bit. Everybody will have his say about opponents and discuss theories on how best to dismiss them. How Andrew Strauss tends to hook in the air square of the wicket or that Kevin Pietersen is particularly strong on the on-side. I'm just not that interested in observations like this. Even less so when they're coming from our bus driver.

A few of us tried grabbing a quick bite out tonight but it was just about impossible. Cricket fans were everywhere and we couldn't walk into a restaurant or pub without a dozen people immediately lining up for autographs. Not that I'm complaining! Being recognised and always asked to sign things comes with the territory. And I'm generally pretty happy to oblige. About the only time this sort of public attention has ever got to me was a few years back when my Dad was in hospital. I'd go in to visit him every few days and we'd be sitting there having a chat when someone would poke their head into the ward asking me to sign a shirt or a hat or a bat. Like I said, I rarely knock anyone back, but I felt this was kind of overstepping the mark so, in the end, I had a word with the hospital's head doctor. He was very embarrassed, and promised to do something about it, in return for a signed top.

The rest of the evening was spent dealing with email requests, many from organisations seeking my help with fundraising. I tell you what, if I only had a dollar for every bloody charity ball or black tie dinner I've hosted! It's got so bad that these days I've reluctantly started charging for my services, but at a greatly reduced rate of course. I'm hardly about to sting some kids cancer group for top dollar, but there are expenses, such as petrol and dry cleaning (you'd be amazed at what gets spilt on a celebrity MC). Tonight I have been asked to host some sort of charity golf day in October. Normally I would be away but, as it turns out, this year's CARM (Cricketers As Role Models) tour has been called off after one of our team leaders was picked up for drink-driving, so I said 'yes', subject to availability and finding out what the group does.

29 Wednesday

One of the boys pointed out an interesting clue that appeared in the *Guardian* crossword yesterday.

4 Dastardly, making heavy weather (7,2)
5 No one at home, try listening (3,4)
6 Alcohol in heated cricketer (2,5)
7 That's the girl! Not difficult but sharp (6,3)

The answer turned out to be 'hot toddy' which could be a reference to me. We're not sure, but my manager has agreed to check it out and, if necessary, issue legal proceedings.

Training the day before a Test is generally considered optional, but with so many guys pushing for selection just about all of the squad turned out for today's final session. Due to the appalling weather it was held at Edgbaston's indoor nets centre under the watchful eye of Vinny, Punter and selector-on-duty Jamie Cox. Apart from working on your own form, I find that net sessions are also a good opportunity to point out problems your team-mates might not know they have. For example, just before the Second Test at Lords I mentioned to Snorks how he was shuffling at the crease and cramping himself up. He hadn't actually realised this but, sure enough, he was out for a duck just a few days later, running out of room going for a pull shot. Lucky I said something.

The two blokes most under the pump right now are obviously Boof and Mitch. Our embattled speedster spent the morning working with bowling coach Troy Cooley and looked to be regaining his rhythm and pace. From what I saw Mitch should be right for tomorrow's match. And, if not, we could simply ask Cools to play.

The news regarding Boof was not so positive. Although there's been nothing official said so far about him missing out on selection, I have heard rumours from a very highly placed source (a marketing manager at Victoria Bitter) that his position may be in jeopardy. And, sure enough, this afternoon it was confirmed – Boof is out. Telling a player he's dropped is never easy, which is why we tend to leave it to journos, but this time Punter and Vinny decided to deliver the news in person. Boof took it surprisingly well and I just know a bloke of his talent will bounce back. Or retire and write a tell-all exposé about his unjustified shafting. Either way, he'll make a success of it.

Of course, one bloke's bad luck is another bloke's opportunity and Watto learned today that he will step in as our new opener. The big Queenslander was understandably elated and celebrated the news in typical fashion – face down on the physio's bench receiving treatment for a back niggle. The real test now will be getting him and Katto talking. Communication between opening batsmen is obviously vital but unfortunately these two have not even been speaking to each other following a dispute that arose during one of last week's team bonding exercises. But I'm sure they will be able to sort things out.

During breaks in the weather a few of us took the opportunity to inspect the Edgbaston pitch. I tell you what, you'd have more chance of holding the World Swimming Championships here than a first-class cricket match.

Details of an interesting media stoush emerged today, involving a falling out between Matthew Hayden and Geoff Boycott who are both over here working for the BBC. Haydos apparently quipped that Boycott's batting style 'emptied cricket grounds', prompting Boycott to immediately storm out saying, 'I don't need comments like that at my age.' He was eventually convinced to return (luckily a listener's cake had just arrived) and they both shook hands later, but the atmosphere is still said to be a little frosty.  This incident reminded me of the time I was doing commentary for Foxtel and I jokingly mentioned that the pitch was 'as dry and lifeless as Greg Matthews' scalp', only to have 'Mo' burst into the box and threaten to 'punch my lights out'. I naturally apologised but we haven't really spoken since.

At tonight's meeting Punt and Vinny gathered us all together. Their message was simple. After all the training and preparation, this was it, the time for talk was over. Why, then, they both spoke for another hour and a half remains unclear, but there was quite a bit to get through. The main thing we needed to address was team unity and, to do this, we broke up into groups. After coming back together we ran through the usual tactical points and then Punter did something quite interesting. He got up and gave each member of the team a pen and paper, telling us to answer the question 'How can I improve as a player?' Half an hour later I handed him several pages of detailed notes outlining flaws in both his batting technique and various aspects of his recent captaincy. He seemed a little under-appreciative.

Despite what some purists might say, sledging (or the gentle art of verbal harassment) is as much a part of modern cricket as random drug testing and player payment disputes. And, if a fielding side thinks it can unsettle a batsman with a few well-chosen words while he's at the crease, then I see nothing wrong with it.

Of course, when it comes to insulting an opponent there is a line that we know not to cross and we are bound to avoid making any comment that ridicules a player's race, religion, skin colour or choice of footwear sponsor. On the other hand, his talent, appearance, recent record, wife/girlfriend/mother and erectile competency are considered open targets.

Racial intolerance has no place on the cricket field and I favour a zero-tolerance approach, especially when it comes to Indian and Pakistani players who, let's face it, are notorious for this sort of thing.

The trick is to work out who might be vulnerable to a few well-chosen words. Some players are simply unphased by chirping (as the South Africans call it) and you're pretty much wasting your time. I remember when I first played in a Test against Sachin Tendulkar; we spent the entire day right in his face. Didn't trouble him one bit, so we were then forced to change tactics. Gave him four days of the 'silent treatment' but by then it was too late and the 'little master' had settled into a groove. The other thing I've learnt is that it's far more effective to make the odd comment here and there than to try and maintain a continual flow. It's also less exhausting. And, while direct abuse works well in some situations ('mate, you bat like a girl') it's sometimes more unsettling to weave your comments into natural sounding conversations ('hey BJ have you noticed how this bloke bats like a complete girl?'). Indirect but equally devastating.

In the old days you could pretty much say what you wanted, safe in the knowledge that any comments would stay on the field. But these days television cameras are on you constantly and people can often lip read. So I generally wait 'til the end of an over if I want to say something particularly strong. Even then, some networks get sneaky and keep the tape rolling, only to replay your 'conversation' as part of a lunchtime highlights package.

If you ask me it's unfair when sides sledge in foreign languages. Afrikaans or Urdu. I learnt a bit of French at school but the Frogs don't play cricket and – even if they did – the best I could manage would be telling them to do something unpleasant to their aunt with a pen. Not much help to anyone.

Sledging is about getting under a batsman's skin. Throwing his concentration. But it should never be personal or cruel. If, for example, a bloke walks out to the middle and you know he has just lost a family member or had someone close to him diagnosed with a serious illness, you wouldn't say that while he was taking guard. Mind you, if he got to 50-plus and looked like going on with it you might consider a couple of passing references.

30 Thursday

England v Australia (Third Test)
Edgbaston
Day 1

Arriving at the ground, things didn't look all that promising. Heavy overnight rain had left the field waterlogged and, despite constant pitch inspections, the surface was deemed unfit to play on. This meant we had to sit in the rooms for most of the day listening to the Barmy Army rehearsing their latest repertoire of anti-Australian chants. That said, I must say they're certainly a professional unit; I'm sure I even heard a couple of key changes in some of the longer songs. We passed the time just playing cards and waiting for some sort of announcement. Finally a start time of 4.45 pm was given, which we then succeeded in having pushed back 10 minutes because Katto was sitting on a straight flush.

After sitting on our bums all day it was important that everyone warmed up properly. Of course, we do this before any game, heading out into the middle for fielding drills, throw-downs and various stretches. These pre-match sessions are quite extensive and carefully planned, which certainly makes a change from when I first started playing cricket. Back then a warm-up meant dumping your gear in the corner of the room, plugging in the urn and looking for an ashtray.

Team meetings are important, but so too are calls from your manager about a potential IPL contract.

It was during this afternoon's warm-ups that disaster struck, with our wicket-keeper somehow managing to break his finger. Details remain sketchy but it seems that BJ and Sidds were out in the middle taking some catches when Sidds threw one in hard and low, hitting him on the tip of his finger. BJ immediately collapsed in pain, prompting Sidds to immediately appeal (it was an automatic response) at which point we all realised something had happened. People came from everywhere, including our physio, coaches, support staff and even the official photographer (who wanted to know if he had to do another team portrait). In the end it was up to BJ to make one of those really tough decisions. No bloke wants to give up his place in the side, but if you know you're not up to five days in the field, better to say so up front rather than risk letting the team down. Anyway, BJ did the right thing and agreed to withdraw, meaning our reserve keeper would have to step in, and the next thing we knew selector Jamie Cox was saying, 'Choco, get your whites on mate, you're playing.' I don't know who was more shocked; us, or the room attendant he was inadvertently speaking to (Choco was out the back at the time organising drinks). Of course, the drama didn't end there. We then had to get the Poms to agree to our late team change (they did) and organise a new baggy green for Choco (turns out Brute has half a dozen blank caps in his briefcase). With no distinguished past player around to preside over the presentation we got our bus driver to present it. All this excitement and not a ball bowled!

By the time the two captains walked out to toss, the noise was absolutely deafening. Edgbaston is renowned as a cauldron to play in and, even sitting in the rooms, the spectators can be clearly heard letting the visiting team know they're not welcome. The only plus is that when the crowd get to fever pitch they just about drown out the sound of Bing playing his guitar. Punter called the toss correctly and chose to bat, with Katto and Watto getting us off to a good start, taking the score to 86 without loss. This was our biggest opening stand for the series and, being a superstitious lot, no one watching on in the rooms wanted to move in case it jinxed us. I don't think I've spent so long sitting on a toilet since my last tour of India. Eventually Katto was trapped in front by Swann for 46 but Punter played well, taking us to 1/126 by the close of play. A solid result and one we hope to really build on tomorrow.

Winning a Test match is so important to an Australian side that we join arm in arm and sing the team song, often for hours on end. This is a truly special time, not to mention one of the few occasions when players are legally allowed to touch each other. The words are simple, and known to all of us (although Hilfy and Sidds will often ask for the lyrics to be written out on cards).

After play on Day 3, I learned I was on report for 'showing dissent'. What, so now you're not allowed to put your hands on your hips? Unfortunately for me, the report was filed by umpire Aleem Dar so I'll have to tread carefully. It's one thing to walk away with a match fine, but no one wants a fatwah hovering over them.

Christmas capers

Christmas on the eve of the Boxing Day Test in Melbourne has always been a special time for the Australian cricket team. It's then that we gather our immediate family, friends, fellow players and major sponsors for a yuletide celebration. It's a traditional affair – held at Crown Casino – and it's wonderful to watch the kids running round, eating lollies and tearing presents open. Naturally there are always a few tantrums (I remember 2008 when Michael Clarke had to be sent off for an afternoon nap) but I wouldn't miss it for the world.

As part of the series build-up we players all got to pose for a photo with the famous Ashes urn. Well, a replica of the Ashes urn as the real item is considered far too fragile to be handled. 'Bit like Watto!' I quipped to the local press. Watto didn't take it well and, as a result, we've spent the entire tour sitting at opposite ends of the team bus.

While I'm more than happy to help Punter set fields, there's not much I can do if he chooses to ignore my advice.

Running between wickets – Toddy's Take

You have to laugh at the way some younger players sprint between wickets, convinced that every single can be turned into two, every two into three. Take some advice from an experienced campaigner. Pace yourself. There's no point in running so hard that you've barely got enough breath to face the next delivery. I prefer a gentle trot although I will, if my batting partner is in danger of being run out, break into a jog. Anything more is just showing off.

After a victory there's nothing wrong with walking off with a few souvenirs. In addition to the stumps and ball I managed to grab umpire Koertzen's watch.

Beach cricket – Toddy's Take

While some may look down their noses at it, the XXXX Gold Beach Cricket competition is an exciting format and, personally, I think it's disappointing that this form of the game is yet to be accorded first-class status. Okay, it's not Test cricket but the fans love it. And what's not to like? Seeing great athletes such as Junior, Flem, Dizzy, Boof, Deano and Yours Truly in peak physical condition (not to mention yellow speedos) wielding the willow on beaches all around Australia. There's even talk of beach cricket becoming an Olympic sport to replace handball or one of the less interesting women's cycling events. I say 'bring it on!'

THE Daily Star

Tuesday, July 28, 2009   **30p**   www.thedailystar.co.uk

Pub Punch-on!
Todd caught up in bar room brawl

Birmingham, UK: Australian batsman Warwick Todd was today called upon by team management to answer questions about an ugly incident that allegedly took place at a local hotel.

Getting into a fight outside a UK pub was deemed a 'breach of Cricket Australia's code of conduct'. I argued that, as the bloke I hit wasn't actually Australian, the code did not apply, but this defence was rejected.

Uncalled-for comments

In recent times there has been a growing trend for ex-players who find themselves writing for newspapers or on radio making increasingly outlandish comments about members of the current squad. They'll write about 'spats' between players that never took place, or dressing room 'incidents' that none of us have even heard of. One of the most outrageous  claims in recent times has been that Punter and I don't get along! To back this claim up they'll point to so-called 'confrontations' on the field, such as the two of us having an animated conversation with a lot of arm waving. All we're probably doing is discussing field placements. I know for a fact that Punter values my contribution in this area. Sure, he may not always follow my advice and – as a result – end up setting an incorrect field, but after a few balls have been struck through the *very gap* I warned him about he usually sees the light and comes round to my way of thinking. But as for 'not getting on'? It's absolute crap and just another example of shoddy journalism.

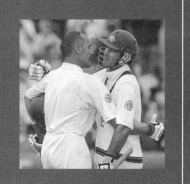

July

31 Friday

England v Australia (Third Test)
Edgbaston
Day 2

I'm sitting in my room, it's 10.30 pm and I'm trying to make sense of what happened today and all I can do is come up with one word. Onions. Together with Anderson and the other English bowlers he completely destroyed us. We were outplayed in all facets of the game. I'm trying to find one positive from today and the best I can come up with is lunch.

The day began badly when Watto went without adding to his overnight score of 62, missing a straight one from Onions. Then Huss was bowled the very next ball not playing a shot to a ball that *looked* like it was going straight on – and then did. You should have heard the noise! The stadium absolutely erupted as the crowd went wild, sensing an Aussie collapse. What you need in these times of crisis is for one player to put his hand up and that's exactly what Punter did, gloving one from Onions through to the keeper. When Pup went for just 29 I knew it was time for someone to stand up and be counted.

I tell you what, those first few overs were not easy. The ball was seaming wildly, the bowlers fired up and the crowd noise almost overwhelming. But I simply made a point of getting in behind the line and really concentrating. The key was picking the ball; not being deceived by flight or speed. Experienced batsmen can often tell what sort of ball is about to be bowled simply by focusing on the bowler's body language. There are often small, tell-tale signs. The raising of an elbow or subtle shifting of a wrist. Of course, some bowlers are easier to pick than others. Sidds, for example, will often give away the fact he is about to bowl a bouncer by waving to Punter at slip and shouting 'I'm about to bowl a bouncer'. Onions was trickier to read, but I managed to do so, advancing to my first half-century of the tour. I really wanted to go on and make a ton but on 54 I yet again fell victim to some poor umpiring. The ball went down leg-side and despite not having my bat or gloves anywhere near it the umpire deemed that it had somehow made contact. I honestly couldn't believe it and stood there stunned for what seemed like a few seconds (but later proved to be six and a half minutes) before heading back to the rooms. At moments like this you know that every camera at the ground is trained directly at you so it's important not to let your face show any sign of emotion or anger. Although the sight of my bat arcing through the air and into an advertising hoarding may have given the game away.

Shortly after lunch our last wicket fell with the total on just 263. Not a great score but certainly one we could defend. Hilfy took the new ball and opened with a maiden and then Sidds got Cook in the very next over. This was a big wicket for our reserve keeper Choco, his first in Test cricket, and all the boys came in to congratulate him, some using the opportunity to actually introduce themselves at the same time (there really hadn't been much socialising up until this point of the tour).

But from then on we struggled. Strauss was particularly brutal, racing to his half-century and, by the time bad light stopped play, England were 2/116 and closing in fast.

In the field

When fielding close to the batsman, it's vital to keep up a steady stream of comments that not only pump your bowlers up but also make the batsman feel he's always on the verge of losing his wicket. Here are some typical Aussie expressions you're likely to hear, and when.

Oooooh! = the ball passed within half a metre of the stumps
Aaaaaagh! = the ball landed on the pitch
Earrggghh = the batsman played and missed
Aeaeaerrrgh = Punter's just swallowed his gum
Catch it! = the batsman made contact (this expression should be used even if the ball is rolling along the ground)
Howizeeeee? = the batsman swung and missed
Well bowled (insert bowler's name here) = the batsman just hit a six
Yes! = nothing's happened but the bowler's looking dispirited
One early! = general encouragement for the team to pick up an early wicket (not to be used after the first drinks break or it starts to sound silly).

August

1 Saturday

England v Australia (Third Test)
Edgbaston
Day 3

Alright, I'll admit that yesterday was not our finest day on a cricket field, but to hear some of the rubbish being said about us right now you'd think we were trailing by 600 runs! One so-called 'expert' went as far as to say that Australia has 'gone soft, lost that mongrel, aggressive edge that made us feared by other teams'. Unbelievable. A few of the boys talked about issuing a public response, but in the end we decided we didn't want to upset anyone.

Despite our poor form on the scoreboard there was still quite a fuss made yesterday about Punter overtaking AB to become Australia's all-time highest run scorer. A few of the guys were asked for a comment after play and Pup started talking our skipper up as 'the greatest since Bradman'. I was a little less over the top, simply saying that it was a 'fine effort' – Punter told us all days ago he didn't want a fuss made. Turns out now he's pissed off I didn't say more.

In terms of play there's not much to report as the entire day was officially rained out. The umpires conducted pitch inspections at 10.45 am, 12.00 pm, 1.30 pm and 2.30 pm before finally agreeing to officially abandon play at 2.40 pm. And things are not looking much better for tomorrow. Radar images from the weather bureau show there may be a brief break in the rain clouds but, unfortunately, this is currently located over Madrid.

Long tours –Toddy's Take

It can get very lonely on the road, when you spend all your time at cricket grounds and in hotel rooms day after day while your family is back home. I have had nights on long tours when the temptation to jump in a cab to the airport and fly home has been almost overwhelming. And the only thing that's stopped me has been a sense of loyalty to the team, or the fact we've got a poker game going and I'm on a roll.

Smokin' – Toddy's Take

Much has been written about my long (and often unsuccessful!) battle to give up the fags. It can't be denied, smoking is a disgusting habit and bad for not just the smoker, but those around him too. I was always conscious of this when the kids where young and, if I wanted a smoke, it was time to go outside. Sure, I didn't feel good about making them stand out in the cold and the rain, but it was for their own wellbeing. Anyway, when the folks at Nicoquit approached me to endorse their new super strength gum I was keen to give it a go. And, I could honestly say that thanks to Nicoquit I was soon down to 39 cigarettes a day (from 40, so it's hardly a glowing endorsement).

August

England v Australia (Third Test)
Edgbaston
Day 4

A pitch inspection at 11.00 this morning revealed the ground to still be wet but playable and a delayed start was scheduled for 12.00 pm. It was also agreed that 91 overs were to be bowled, which given our record of no-balls could well have seen us here 'til midnight.

As usual we had a quick warm-up and then gathered in the rooms for a final chat. It was here that the Plan and Theme group announced they had changed their theme for today to Courage after being convinced by Vinny that their original theme (We're Stuffed) may have been a little defeatist.

Before taking the field, Punter gathered us all in a circle and asked each player to say a few words about what it meant being part of the Australian team, to represent your country at the game's highest level. I heard afterwards that a few people thought my speech was not entirely appropriate, in particular the way I took the opportunity to acknowledge several major commercial sponsors, but I feel this is just being picky. The folks at True-G Mobile are equally important to my journey as a cricketer as anyone else and getting everyone to sing along to their jingle seemed a great way to kick off the day.

Hilfy and Sidds took the ball and the big Tasmanian broke through after a few overs, getting rid of Strauss for 69 before picking up Collingwood in the last over before lunch. But despite these key wickets, the runs kept flowing and Punter was forced to try various bowling options including Ritzy, Snorks and myself. Noticeable by his absence was Mitch who seemed clearly out of favour with our captain. I tell you what, there's nothing more excruciating than watching a bowler who thinks he should be given the ball try and drop hints to his skipper. It generally starts with a few shoulder rolls, but if that doesn't do the trick he'll often move on to upper body stretches and abdominal crunches. By mid-morning Mitch was on the ground attempting one-armed push-ups before Punter finally acknowledged him with a few overs. And the big Queenslander came close to breaking through. It was in the 49th over, Bell miscued and the ball thudded into Katto who was fielding at short leg, only to have it bounce off him and hit the ground. That's why Boonie was so effective at this position. If a ball was hit anywhere near his midriff it would be guaranteed to stick in a fold of skin somewhere (often not being found for days).

After lunch Sidds got Prior for 41, caught by Boof who was on the field as sub. But then Flintoff cut loose, making a valuable 74, followed by another few annoying tail-end partnerships that saw England cruise to a total of 376. Not insurmountable, sure, but still a lot. What we really needed was to survive the final session without losing a wicket, and Watto and Katto certainly looked like doing that until Katto got an edge from Onions and was out for 26. Then Punter was bowled by Swann for just 5, extending his disappointing run in this series.

Heading back to the sheds we could tell our captain was not happy and braced ourselves for the worst. Over the years Australian batsmen have vented their frustration at being dismissed in a variety of ways. Pistol once made a duck at The Oval and smashed his bat to pieces – belting it against his coffin until it was just splinters. Bevo took a shower while fully kitted out. Slats expressed his disgust by shoving his bat, pads and gloves into the toilet and attempting to flush them away. In 2004 I responded to being caught in the outfield by dousing my one day uniform in lighter fluid and setting it on fire. It certainly worked well in terms of stress relief, until I got word that the third umpire had over-ruled the decision and I was required back in the middle. I lasted another over before being forced to retire charred. But Punter was remarkably restrained, with only superficial damage being inflicted on a locker and a small section of retaining wall knocked out. Luckily no further wickets fell and we resume tomorrow on 2/88, just 25 runs behind.

When your captain wants you fielding down on the fence in front of the Barmy Army all you can do is pretend not to hear and hope he'll choose someone else.

August

3 Monday

England v Australia (Third Test)
Edgbaston
Day 5

There wasn't much to be said in the rooms before play today. We all knew what was required – some old-fashioned Aussie grit and determination. Like our diggers at Kokoda with their backs to the wall or our volunteer rural fire fighters facing up to a blazing inferno, it was time to tough it out. Punter's advice was for everyone to play their natural game, except for Huss who, given our number 3's recent form, he felt might be better playing someone else's natural game.

As expected, the Poms greeted us with a fiery spell of fast bowling. Watto copped some ferocious blows, one on the forearm from Flintoff and another from Punter when he was out a few balls later trying to hook. Huss went soon after for 64, not a bad score for someone in the middle of a serious form slump. Hopefully this knock will silence some of his harsher critics. I know I'll have to tone things down. In the end it was left to Pup and myself to steady the ship, not an easy task by any means. Batting is a process that involves constant decisions. Every ball that comes your way forces you to ask yourself a series of questions. Should I go forward or go back? Should I play it or leave it? Should I play defensively or aggressively? Should I play on-side or off? In the space of a single over you can easily find yourself having to make 42 decisions, 43 if you're also thinking about lunch. But we managed to do it. Pup reached his century first and celebrated in customary fashion, glancing up to watch himself on the big scoreboard. I followed suit a few overs later, bringing up my ton with a stylish leg glance. I heard later that a few commentators felt I might have got a bit 'carried away' after reaching my century but, if you ask me, there's nothing wrong with kissing your helmet upon reaching such a milestone. Okay, trying to kiss Pup's might have been going a bit far, but I was caught up in the emotion of the moment. He didn't seem to mind.

With 13 overs to go the captains agreed to call off play, leaving the match drawn – a pretty fair result after so much time lost due to rain. Pup was named Man of the Match and I couldn't be happier for him. His knock was pretty classy and even though I've since heard quite a few people mentioning the fact that he had three separate lives that's not something I need to go into here.*

Despite ending in a draw we felt there were many positives to come out of Edgbaston. Centuries to Pup and myself, Watto's strong performance as our new opener and Huss getting a half-century. Plus Mitch looks to be on the improve. All more than enough reason to let our hair down with a decent night out. These events are generally organised by our social committee; unfortunately, this week it's headed up by Huss and, as a result, tonight's activity was a 10-km run followed by an indoor net session under lights. Might be time for a new committee head.

*But I will here. Pup was dropped by Strauss off Bopara on 38, had the ball glance his bails without removing it and then was caught at slip on 96 off a no-ball. Still, I'm sure the Man of the Match committee know what they're doing.

Slumps – Toddy's Take

It can happen to anyone who has ever picked up a cricket bat. A run of low scores, a string of outs, a sense that you've lost that magic touch. And players caught in this sort of slump will resort to just about anything. Some try changing their action, which is always dangerous. Others go on fitness kicks – even worse. While the problem may occasionally be technical, in most cases it's simply the mind playing tricks. True story: Former Australian physio Errol Alcott used to keep a stash of white Smarties in his medical kit. When a batsman was struggling, 'Hooter' would simply administer one of these 'magic' pills and surprise, surprise – form slump over. Warnie's mum used to have a similar supply of pharmaceuticals. If the problem is mental then some players may consider bringing in professional help but, in my experience, this tends to be of limited value. During a rough trot over the 2003–04 season I agreed to speak with a sports psychologist. Several sessions later he identified the problem – I was afraid of intimacy. This came as quite a surprise as I thought my issue was related to backswing.

August

4 Tuesday

Birmingham to Leeds

This morning it was back on the bus for the 180-km trek to Headingley, a trip that turned out to be 225 km after Pup realised he'd left his sunglasses at the hotel and insisted on going back. Last night I wrote in my regular News Limited column that I believed we could (still) win this series, but that it would require a combination of planning, vision, talent, belief, tenacity, consistency, thoroughness, perspicacity, *coeur d'esprit*, positive attitude and team work. (I'm not actually sure what some of those things mean, but when you're under the pump to produce 1200 words a week it's just a question of grabbing the thesaurus and giving it a red hot go.)

Of course, not all commentators have been so positive. Quite a few articles in this morning's paper have pointed out that Australia must win the remaining two Ashes Tests against England if it is to retain its current ICC ranking as the world's best nation. It's a far cry from the glory days of earlier this decade when Australia was out front on the table by a mile. It was during this period that we began calling ourselves the New Invincibles, a reference to Bradman's immortal side. Some cricket lovers felt this was disrespectful so it was agreed that we would stop using the term (and I agreed to get rid of the t-shirts), but there's no denying the awesome strength and depth of that squad. A few years on and things have changed. We've lost Pigeon, Warnie, Haydos and Lang. But I believe there's still real talent in our current line-up and, with a little luck, we can continue as world beaters.

Arriving at Leeds we checked into the hotel. There was the usual guff under my door: a welcome from the manager, a room damages waiver form, and a couple of phone messages saying that various members of my family had died – just the boys having a laugh.

After lunch we headed to the ground for a light workout, mainly just a chance to blow the cobwebs out. One bloke who is definitely on the improve is Mitch. His performance in the Third Test, while not perfect, was a step in the right direction, although I sense he's still a little lacking in confidence. He told me today that he's been working closely with Vinny and Cools who have given him a four-point bowling plan involving run-up, wrist angle, seam position and delivery stride. I took the big paceman aside and gave him my own four-point plan.

1. Get
2. In
3. Their
4. Faces

I think he got the message.

I tell you what, there's a bit of pressure on the team heading into this Fourth Test. We all know that a loss at Headingley will mean the end of our bid to retain the Ashes. But a great Australian author once said, 'When backed into a corner – fight your way out.' And those words are as true today as when Chopper Read first wrote them.

During lunch we had a talk from a visiting sports psychologist about the benefits of positive visualisation. He told us that the mind is a powerful tool and it can influence the way our body works, giving us this example: 'If you think about having sex with a beautiful woman the chances are you'll get an erection.' He went on to explain how this mind–body technique might be applied to benefit us in a sporting context but, to be honest, I don't remember much about this bit – I was still thinking about the beautiful woman.

Speaking of women, quite a few of the guys without partners over here at the moment are enjoying the company of some rather enthusiastic local fans and, as a result, are spending a lot of time on the phone, either sending or receiving text messages. My advice to them is simple – be very careful. The old mobile phone has brought more than one sportsman undone over the years. In fact, my old mate Marto's entire wedding fell through when his fiancée apparently found a few 'steamy' exchanges on his phone from someone clearly infatuated with him (it later turned out to be Adam Gilchrist). The point is, it only takes one ru@hotel? to land you in hot water.

Another team meeting was called for this afternoon to discuss tactics for the upcoming Test. I'm sure these sorts of planning sessions have some value. However, if you ask me, cricket is a pretty basic game; you get out in the middle and try to make runs. Sometimes over-analysis can just end up causing confusion. Let's face it, all the computer modelling and wagon wheels in the world won't get you to triple figures. And fast bowlers certainly don't need to start worrying about 'pressure-mounting spells'; as long as they get on the team bus and remember to wear socks, a good captain can pretty much direct things from there.

August

Leeds

Talk about desperate! A group of local English supporters attempted to disrupt our preparation for the Test by assembling out front of the team hotel at dawn this morning armed with horns and whistles. It was a cheap stunt and one that failed to have any real effect as most of the boys were either sleeping at the back of the hotel or not yet back from the nightclub.

With just 48 hours to the start of the Test it was another big day of training and preparation. After a light breakfast I spent an hour and a half in the hotel's fitness centre; 20 minutes doing weights and the rest getting a haircut. Then it was down to the ground for a net session and fielding drills. By this stage of the tour a lot of the boys have their managers over here and things can get a little crowded, especially in the nets when a few of them insist on helping out with batting practice.

There's been a fair bit of talk in the press about the hostile crowd reaction we faced at Edgbaston, in particular the Barmy Army who kept up a steady stream of anti-Australian musical sentiments. Some commentators felt that it was a little 'over the top' but to be honest I'm not fussed. I thrive on hostile reactions and I frankly couldn't care less if a group of people decide they don't like me (unless they're members of a jury hearing my drink-drive charge, in which case I might try and win them over). Of course, there's a fine line between good-natured stirring and unacceptable behaviour. While most crowds are generally quite reasonable, there have been times when some have overstepped the mark. Back in 2001 at Trent Bridge a firework narrowly missed Bing, prompting us to leave the field. On another occasion during a presentation ceremony at Lords, Bevo was struck on the side of the head with a beer can (the culprit was eventually identified and never played for Australia again). But these are rare examples and we don't expect any such trouble at Headingley.

Another good, intense net session for everyone this morning. By this stage of the tour most of the guys have settled into a training routine; they know what's expected of them. As an experienced and senior member of the squad I am always happy to share my knowledge with the younger blokes. If they're struggling, I'll remind them of the fact. If they're doing well I'll keep quiet – no point in any of them getting a big head.

One bloke clearly keen to impress the selectors was Bing, who produced a fiery spell of fast bowling in the nets. If you ask me, the key with Bing is to not over-bowl him; he is at his most effective when used in short, sharp bursts. You bring him on for, say, the first 10 overs then not again until the following summer.

Our other injured squad member is of course BJ who, after receiving a pain-killing injection, completed his first training session today. The good news is that he doesn't feel any pain in his finger. The worrying news is he can't feel anything from the waist up, so it may be a question of cutting back a little on the dose.

Of course, England are not without fitness worries of their own. Lords hero Freddy Flintoff continues to battle a serious knee injury and there's talk of him bowling in this Test wearing a specially designed brace. What's so special about this brace no one can say but the Poms regard it as so important that it's apparently been given its own hotel room.

Back at the hotel Vinny and Punter called us together for a chat about the upcoming Test. Some of the guys complained, saying that we're having too many meetings, and so a meeting has been called tomorrow to discuss the issue.

On a long tour such as this, trust is very important. Sadly, I felt that trust was breached tonight when we were told to report to the hotel conference room at 7.30 pm sharp for a 'very special surprise'. Sensing a free feed and the possibility of an open bar, most of the guys walked in right on time. Turned out to be another bat signing session.

If that wasn't enough to get me in a bad mood, I got back to my room only to find an email this evening from Neville advising me that I have been officially banned by ABC Radio from calling any future games. This issue goes back to last summer when I did a stint as special commentator on ABC *Grandstand*. While I felt my contribution was quite valuable there were, apparently, several complaints that I had somehow breached their rules on 'commercial endorsements'. For the record, I was not 'endorsing' any particular brand of energy drink. I merely mentioned how much this particular one often helped my on-field performances and the fact that it was available on special at a range of selected outlets. And then I hummed a few bars of the jingle. Talk about sensitive. Anyway, I've now been blacklisted, which is a real pity but I'm not going to let it get me down.

August

6 Thursday

Leeds

We kicked off our final training session this morning with an enjoyable game of touch football that certainly brought out everyone's competitive spirits. As a result there were a few minor injuries, and several blokes who wouldn't talk to each other for the rest of the day. Then it was into the nets for everyone to have one final chance at staking their claim for selection. The most likely move will be Sarfraz in for either Sidds or Haurie.

We were joined at training today by a small group of junior players, all students at the Commonwealth Bank Centre of Excellence back in Brisbane, who are over here to get a taste of touring as international cricketers. I'm a big supporter of the Academy* and have spoken there on several occasions. Let's face it, these young kids will one day be taking our place in the squad, and anything I can do to delay that process is worth the effort. Coaching is something I could easily see myself doing in the future. I think I've got a real skill when it comes to analysing other player's deficiencies, and I take great pleasure in pointing them out. Of course, these days coaching is a little more scientific than when I was first learning the basics and at the Academy they rely heavily on technology. When I was last there they had just installed a new sledging machine. Similar to a bowling machine, you stand in front of it and have pre-recorded insults hurled towards you at high speed and volume. (No one could say who the taped voice belonged to but the rumour was it's Pigeon.)

On a long tour such as this it's important that every member of the group feels valued, not just those of us who are actually playing in the team. It's for this reason that we will often hold social events where people such as our support staff, administrative officials and Cricket Australia representatives are invited to come in at the end and share any food that's left over. Tonight it took the form of a casual barbecue where we got to relax before the start of hostilities tomorrow. One bloke who won't be around to see the match is Ronnie who flies home to Melbourne tonight to be at the birth of his first child. While I'm all for husbands supporting their partners during these special events, I'm not convinced you actually have

---

*My only complaint about the Centre is its current practice of allowing foreign players to come out and train there. I'm all for helping out those in developing countries (I sponsor a kiddie in Auckland) but we don't want foreigners learning about our training methods and drills. How to purify water and fight malaria, maybe. But the reverse sweep? That's classified information.

to be there in person. When Ros was having our first child I simply phoned her from Cape Town to wish her good luck. For our second I sent flowers and a signed bat. In the end it's the thought that counts.

There's an amazing spirit amongst the team right now, a real sense that we can not only win this Test, but go on and claim the series. Make no mistake, confidence is a key factor in sporting success. In fact, most studies show that performance is 30% physical and 60% mental. (The remaining 10% is derived from energy drinks.)

It's one thing to talk big; anyone can do that. But for me, the defining quality of a champion is to walk out there, confront your demons, face up to the knockers and make the game your own. Then write a book about it. Tomorrow we face our greatest test of the tour so far. Sitting in bed I took out my diary and wrote these words:

The best thing in the world is to play and win.
The second best is to play and lose, as long as you are still playing.
The third is to not play but to at least have a bet on the result.

The sheds – Toddy's Take

'What's it like being in Australian dressing rooms?' I wish I had a dollar for every time I've been asked that question! Arguably I have, if you count the number of tour diaries, behind-the-scenes memoirs and tell-all exposés I've managed to pen, not to mention the thousands of after-dinner speeches I've given during which I'll answer questions from the audience. But there's still a certain mystery. The dressing room is our inner sanctum. Just as a judge has his chambers or the President his Oval Office so, too, do we have our dressing room. It's a special place, reserved solely for players, coaches, medical staff, trainers and key footwear sponsors. And it's where we members of the squad can truly relax. It's like our home, only better because we're allowed to put our feet on the furniture. I love it.

August

7 Friday

England v Australia (Fourth Test)
Headingley
Day 1

As has happened so often during this series there was drama a-plenty before a ball had even been bowled. No sooner had we arrived at the ground than we got the news that England hero Freddie Flintoff had been ruled out of the team after his knee failed to respond to treatment, which included pain-killers, ice baths, acupuncture and a personal laying on of hands by the Archbishop of Canterbury. This late withdrawal was followed by another, even later line-up change when England's keeper Matt Prior suffered a severe back spasm in a game of football during their warm-ups. Suddenly England were short a wicket-keeper and, at their request, the toss was pushed back 10 minutes giving Prior just enough time to recover and take his place.

Our team changes were slightly less dramatic but no less exciting for Stuey Clark who came into the side in place of Ritzy. It was a well-deserved recall for the big all-rounder who actually learnt of his inclusion via a Twitter alert from Boof.

When the coin was eventually tossed, England called correctly and elected to bat. Strauss somehow survived a big shout from Hilfy for lbw off the very first ball, an outrageously bad decision from umpire Billy Bowden. I know you've got to give a batsman the benefit of the doubt – but none of us had any doubt that he was out. As it happened Strauss got an edge from Sidds a few balls later. Then Hilfy got Bell, Mitch took care of Bopara with a vicious bouncer and Sarfraz chimed in to remove Collingwood. A few balls later, Cook got what appeared to be an edge but the umpire was not convinced, despite the fact that all of us around the bat had distinctly heard a snick. Even Snorks, who was fielding in the deep, came running in explaining that he was too far away to hear anything but was willing to say he had if it would help. That's the kind of team spirit we had going. The appeal was turned down but it didn't matter because Sarfraz broke through a few overs later. The only real resistance came from Broad who dug in briefly but towards the end of the morning session managed to turn defeat into lunch thanks to another great ball from Sarfraz.

As predicted, the home crowd was pretty pumped up, with the Barmy Army keeping up a steady stream of vocal taunts and jeers. Now we Aussies all enjoy a laugh, but chants like 'Sheep f*#king convicts' and 'Toddy's a wanker' are simply not funny, and verge on being abusive. Realising this was starting to get to us, team management came up with an idea a few days back to enlist the help of the many Australian supporters over here (the Fanatics) by getting them to also sing along at the ground and hopefully drown out the Poms. Unfortunately the idea proved more tricky than first thought. For a start, no one could think of any appropriate Aussie songs. First choices were something by Barnsey or Farnsey, but it turned out both of them were actually born in the UK. Eventually a selection of suitably patriotic anthems was drawn up ('True Blue', 'Come on Aussie Come on', 'Howzat'), and lyrics distributed to anyone wearing green or gold, but this also proved to be a total failure. For a start, none of them could actually sing, let alone hold a tune. By mid-morning today all we were hearing wafting across the outfield was the chorus 'You're going home in the back of a divvy van' chanted over and over again. Not entirely sure how that was supposed to lift our spirits.

But as things turned out it didn't really matter because we managed to wrap the innings up shortly after lunch; England all out for just 102. Watto got our innings off to a flying start, hitting Anderson for consecutive boundaries. Unfortunately Katto went for a duck in the next over, out to a brute of a delivery from Harmison. This brought Punter to the crease and, as expected, he was greeted with a chorus of boos from the English supporters and a chorus of 'Shaddupa Ya Face' by the Aussies who were by now clearly well out of their depth. But this welcome only served to make our skipper more determined as he went on to compile a gutsy 78. By the time Watto reached his half-century a real sense of calm had returned to the Aussie dressing room. Unfortunately, so too had Huss, out for just 10. But we managed to reach 196 without further loss, leaving us in an excellent position to push on tomorrow. And I, for one, can't wait …

August

8 Saturday

England v Australia (Fourth Test)
Headingley
Day 2

Blue skies this morning meant that there was no chance of England being let off the hook through bad weather.

We continued our fine batting form thanks to Pup and Snorks who really kept the scoreboard ticking over. Not that it was easy out there – Harmison was really generating some fierce pace and he managed to crack Pup on the helmet and then the glove with the very next delivery. I tell you, anyone who says they like to face genuine fast bowling is either crazy, lying or Mike Hussey. Just after the first drinks break we lost another wicket, meaning it was time for W.D. Todd to enter the battle. After all the crap written about me in recent weeks and the questioning of my place in the team I set out to respond in the best way I know how; with my bat. In hindsight, smashing a window in the media centre on the way to the crease may not have been the most sensible thing to do, but jeez it felt good, and helped ground me for the innings ahead.

I've heard stories of sportspeople suddenly reaching new heights, performing on a higher plane. Basketballers call it playing 'in the zone'. Cyclists call it EPO. Whatever the case, today something just clicked and, from the very first ball, I felt in total control. Of course, it wasn't easy. By this stage the pitch was starting to break up and the ball was moving about wildly. The bounce got so unpredictable that Graeme Swann decided to field wearing a helmet complete with grille – and he was down on the fence at long on. I could tell that Snorks was struggling a little and, as senior member of the partnership, I took the opportunity between overs to give him some advice. I said, 'Mate, it doesn't matter what these bastards chuck at us as long as we Aussies hold our heads high.' Which is exactly what he did, copping a fearsome blow to the helmet a few balls later when he failed to get under a short one from Anderson. I made it to 86 and was really hoping to go onto three figures when I was given out lbw to a ball that was clearly pitching outside the line.

We made it to 455 all out at tea, giving ourselves one session to get stuck into the opposition. As you'd expect, Punter set a really attacking field, with everyone in their specialist positions; himself and Pup in slips,

When you get hit

Showing pain is a sign of weakness. No matter how much you're hurting, get up quickly and let the bowler know you're fine. Grin, make a joke with your batting partner. Stem any blood flow and, if you suspect a bone may have been broken, avoid even looking at the area. If absolutely necessary (i.e. you've stopped breathing or lost a kidney) call for the physio, but make sure to pretend it's just a change of gloves.

In an effort to make sure a player's injuries are not blown out of proportion by media commentators, here is a list of typical descriptions and their medical definition:

Minor Discomfort = torn muscle or ligament
Discomfort = traumatic dislocation of major joint
Twinge = fracture
Tweak = compound fracture
Niggle = partial loss of brain and/or heart function
Recurrent Niggle = total and permanent paralysis
Strain = life support
Stiffness = death

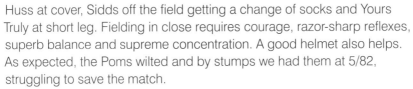

Huss at cover, Sidds off the field getting a change of socks and Yours Truly at short leg. Fielding in close requires courage, razor-sharp reflexes, superb balance and supreme concentration. A good helmet also helps. As expected, the Poms wilted and by stumps we had them at 5/82, struggling to save the match.

All up, a great day, apart from my dubious lbw dismissal. And to make matters worse, I found out after play that not only was the delivery pitching well outside the stumps, but the TV replays have shown it was also a no-ball! Still, that's cricket, and you have to learn to accept the good decisions with the bad. Tomorrow's another day and it's time to move on.

August

Sunday

England v Australia (Fourth Test)
Headingley
Day 3

It's not just that the ball was never going to hit leg stump but the fact I was so far forward there's no way anyone could reasonably give me out. I guess umpire Rauf must have it in for me.

Turned out the Poms have registered an official complaint regarding the last session yesterday, claiming that we were 'over-appealing' (as opposed to over-complaining I guess). Their main target was, no surprises, W. Todd – they claim I was pressuring the umpire with my 'constant' shouts. What crap. I may be a fierce competitor, but I'm also a fair one. And I know for a fact that I'll only appeal if I genuinely believe a batsman is out, or could be out, or should be out.

We began the day, as always, with a quick team meeting during which Punter made it clear that the worst thing we could do is get ahead of ourselves, to start thinking about a victory before we'd even got there. We all agreed and, after a quick discussion about potential venues for our team victory celebrations, we hit the field. The two not-out batsmen were Anderson and Prior. Anderson had apparently hurt his leg going for a quick single yesterday and so was batting with the aid of a runner. While we have no problems with that, we were a little unhappy that the person used was not wearing proper pads or other protective gear. When you act as runner for someone else the rule is you have to carry a bat and wear pretty much what they are wearing: helmet, pads, thigh guards etc. I once ran for Pup in a tour match and was made to get my ear pierced. This bloke was clearly pushing it and we were just about to lodge an official complaint when Hilfy broke through. But then Swann (62) and Broad (61) added what some commentators later called a 'modicum of respect' to England's innings. I don't know what a 'modicum' is, nor do I want to, but let me tell you – there was no 'respect' to be found in England's collapse. Thanks to some inspired bowling from our quicks we had them all out for just 263. No sooner had that last wicket fallen than the party started! Mitch ran off towards cover, arms in the air, triumphant. Punter and Pup high-fived each other. Soon we were all together in a mass team embrace. I honestly don't know how umpire Bowden got caught up in the huddle, but I categorically deny claims that I fondled his buttocks.

August

Singing for our supper

Australian cricketers love to celebrate a win by getting together and singing. This is done after every Test or one-day victory, as well as at the end of a particularly satisfying day off on tour. The song in question has been a source of rich, shared delight for pumped-up Aussie players since the night Rodney Marsh leapt on a dressing-room table and roared four lines he'd picked up from Ian Chappell:

Under the Southern Cross I stand,
A sprig of wattle in my hand,
A native of my native land,
Australia, you f******* beauty.

Marsh did this at the end of the 1972 Oval Test or the 1974 Gabba Test. Memories vary. But the tradition seems to have been bedded down soon after, in Sydney, where a 171-run victory over John Edrich's Englishmen secured for the Australians their long-lost Ashes.

If you ask me, 'Under the Southern Cross' should be our national anthem. Obviously you'd need to replace the 'magic' second last word with something more befitting a ceremonial occasion, but nothing sums up the pride and passion of Australia quite like this humble verse. Even better, there's no actual tune or melody involved, so everyone can join in no matter how pissed.

Under the Southern Cross I stand,
A sprig of wattle in my hand,
A native of my native land,
Australia, you f****** beauty.

(Repeat)
(Repeat again, louder)
(Repeat)
(Repeat until Huss falls off table)

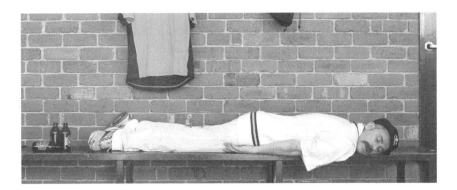

I'm sitting in the dressing room, my gear still on. All around me the boys are celebrating, pouring beer over each other. Punter and BJ have their arms around each other's shoulders. Katto has his hands around Pup's neck, having their usual fight over the song (not over *when* to sing it, but in what key). Why then was I feeling so strangely disconnected? Perhaps because I knew, deep down, that this is the end of the line. Having stepped back into the squad to lend a bit of experience and stability, it was now time for W. Todd to make way for some new blood. In a week or so these boys will be playing for the Ashes. The fifth and deciding Test. And if you'd asked me a few months ago how I thought they'd go, I would have been worried. But over the course of this tour I've seen the Aussie squad go from a bunch of young, eager, super-fit individuals to something much more powerful. A team. Job done. Of course I don't take all the credit for this, there have been a lot of people along the way who have helped out, but I like to feel I've played a part in getting those who wear the baggy green back on track.

Telling the boys was tough. We were in the rooms, soaking in the win, everyone gathered around when I said I was planning to toss it in. I think they were shocked. Not everyone heard because the music was up pretty loud but by the time I made a second announcement the news sunk in. Within minutes word of my retirement got out and my phone lit up with dozens of messages. Some from well-wishers, but mainly friends wanting to see whether they could have my ticket allocation for the Fifth Test.

Few cricketers ever get to plan their retirement. It's something pushed upon them by injury or form. But doing it this way I get to go out at the top of my game. What's more, I do it with a real sense of dignity.

Head lock!

Test star Warwick Todd will be sent home from England in disgrace after assaulting a barman.

CA Chief Executive James Sutherland said last night a drunken Todd became angry when a barman stopped serving drinks. Todd then put the barman in a headlock. He was due to leave Headingley this morning for the flight home. The high-profile player was remorseful but deeply hurt by the severity of the penalty. 'I've done the wrong thing by getting him in a headlock ... it was pretty stupid,' Todd said. 'I'm just glad I didn't hit him. I would have been in more trouble if I'd hit him. A lot more trouble. It was just a headlock. If I wanted to hit him, I would've hit him.' Todd originally denied any wrong-doing, claiming the allegations were made up by people 'who just wanna bring me down'. When informed that the entire incident was captured on video he changed his story, admitting, 'Yeah, it happened then.'

Afterword

I write this short postscript from Delhi, India, where I am currently playing in the Indian Premier League Twenty20 competition. The *Kolkata Cholera* are doing well for a new team, and I really feel I've added something to their batting line-up. My Indian team-mates have, in turn, taught me a lot. I can now sledge fluently in Hindi, Urdu, Punjabi, Tamil and, on special occasions, a mixture of all four.

The 2009 Ashes series did not exactly end as I hoped. Watching the boys fall apart in that Fifth Test was pretty hard to take. And where did they crumble? You guessed it, the middle order. Now I'm not saying that had I been there we would necessarily have won the match, but there's no doubting the absence of W. Todd could well have lost us the Ashes. As it was, my final days in England were pretty frantic. That misunderstanding at the nightclub, followed by the accidental leaking of a dossier I had written in which I said some pretty blunt things about the English team. These comments, intended for private use only, somehow fell into the hands of the local press who described them as 'nasty and vindictive'. All I can say is, thank God they never saw the dossier I wrote about the Australian team. Anyway, it was time to leave.

Since retiring from first-class cricket so many opportunities have opened up for me. Hosting corporate functions, management training seminars, there's even talk of my coaching camps going international. As usual I've had a lot of offers from media organisations wanting me as part of their commentary team. But, to be honest, I'm looking beyond this to more interesting opportunities, ventures that will put something back into the broader community. Like opening my own online betting agency. In terms of TV, I'd love to do something that combines all of my skills and interests. Like being the really nasty judge on a home-brewing reality series where the losing contestant gets a serious send-off. Or perhaps state politics. I could honestly see myself doing anything, provided it was challenging and rewarding – and didn't involve a police check.

What the future holds for W. Todd is hard to say. But I can tell you this, the past 12 months have been an unforgettable journey. I hope you've enjoyed sharing it with me. If there's a message to take from this book, it's simply this – follow your heart. Dream big and never listen to those people who say you can't do something.*

W. Todd
Kolkata, India

*Unless they're nightclub security staff, in which case I've generally found it wise to follow orders.

Index

A note to teachers

Should this book ever become a required text (and it bloody well should be) make sure your students all buy their own copy. Remind them that photocopying bits is illegal and that I will track down those who attempt to do so and hurt them. (Obviously you might want to soften this message for younger kids – just say I'll be really pissed off.)

Other recent titles by Warwick Todd

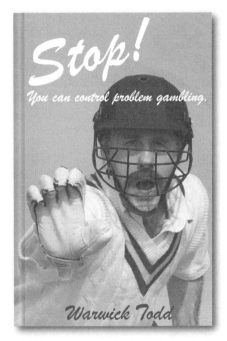

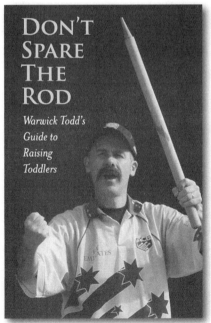

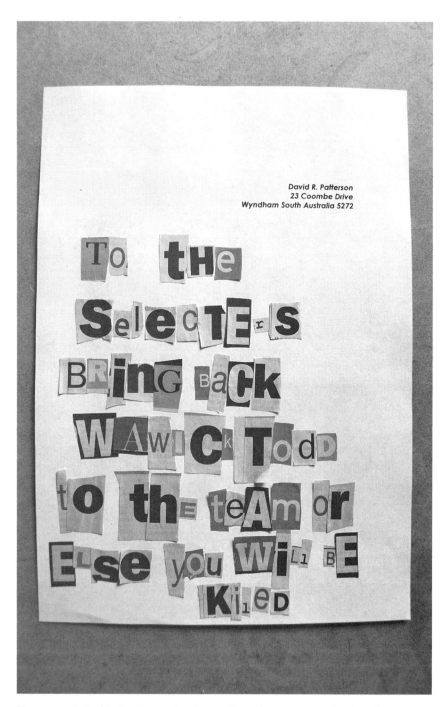

David R. Patterson
23 Coombe Drive
Wyndham South Australia 5272

To the SelecTErs BRinG BaCk WAWiCK ToDD to the teAm or ElSe yOu WiLl BE KiLeD

I have never lacked for loyal supporters. Many of these fans are as passionate as they are mentally unhinged.